A DISCUSSION ON
SLAVEHOLDING

A DISCUSSION ON SLAVEHOLDING

THREE LETTERS TO A CONSERVATIVE,
By
GEORGE D. ARMSTRONG

And

THREE CONSERVATIVE REPLIES,
By
C. VAN RENSSELAER

The Black Heritage Library Collection

BOOKS FOR LIBRARIES PRESS
FREEPORT, NEW YORK
1972

First Published 1858

Reprinted 1972

Reprinted from a copy in the
Fisk University Library Negro Collection

Library of Congress Cataloging in Publication Data

Armstrong, George Dodd, 1813-1899.
    A discussion on slaveholding.

    (The Black heritage library collection)
    Reprint of the 1858 ed.
    1. Slavery in the United States--Controversial
literature--1858. 2. Slavery--Justification.
3. Slavery and the church. I. Van Rensselaer,
Cortlandt, 1808-1860. II. Title. III. Series.
E449.A743 1972   301.44'93'0973   72-6454
ISBN 0-8369-9155-9

PRINTED IN THE UNITED STATES OF AMERICA

A Discussion on Slaveholding.

THREE LETTERS TO A CONSERVATIVE,

BY

GEORGE D. ARMSTRONG, D.D.,

OF VIRGINIA.

AND

THREE CONSERVATIVE REPLIES,

BY

C. VAN RENSSELAER, D.D.,

OF NEW JERSEY.

I. ON THE SCRIPTURAL DOCTRINE OF SLAVEHOLDING.
II. ON EMANCIPATION AND THE CHURCH.
III. ON THE HISTORICAL ARGUMENT FOR SLAVEHOLDING.

TOGETHER WITH

TWO REJOINDERS,

ON SLAVEHOLDING, SCHEMES OF EMANCIPATION, COLONIZATION, ETC.

PHILADELPHIA:
JOSEPH M. WILSON, 111 SOUTH TENTH STREET.
1858.

PREFACE.

THE Letters of Dr. Armstrong to Dr. Van Rensselaer were occasioned by a brief notice of Dr. Armstrong's book "On the Scripture Doctrine of Slavery," in the Presbyterian Magazine for September, 1857.

Dr. Armstrong's Letters originally appeared in the "CENTRAL PRESBYTERIAN," published in Richmond, Va. They were afterwards transferred to the pages of the "PRESBYTERIAN MAGAZINE;" and the Replies by Dr. Van Rensselaer appeared simultaneously with each Letter, in three numbers of that periodical.

The three *Letters* and the three *Replies* were printed in pamphlet form, in April last. But a copy having been sent to Dr. Armstrong before circulation, he objected to the publication of the Series without certain *Rejoinders*, which he proposed to publish in the Presbyterian Magazine, if permitted to do so. Permission was granted; and hence the publication of the pamphlet has been delayed until the Rejoinders and the Replies to them, have been finally issued.

It is due to Dr. Armstrong to say that the delay has been principally owing to circumstances beyond the control of the Editor.

It is also proper to add, for the information of strangers, that both the writers are ministers of the Presbyterian Church (Old School).

DR. ARMSTRONG'S
THREE LETTERS TO A CONSERVATIVE.

LETTER I.

ON THE PROPER STATEMENT OF THE SCRIPTURE DOCTRINE OF SLAVERY.

To the Rev. C. Van Rensselaer, D.D.: The September number of the "Presbyterian Magazine" contains a short review of several recently published works on Slavery, among others, of the " Christian Doctrine of Slavery." In the course of this review you express certain opinions, which, if I mistake not, constitute the peculiar creed of those who take the title of *Conservatives*, as contradistinguished from the *Abolitionist*, on the one hand, and what they designate as the *Pro-slavery man*,* on the other. On these opinions I take the liberty of addressing you thus, through the press.

Do not understand me as intending to find fault with your treatment of my book. The spirit in which you have reviewed it is all that I could desire, and the praise you have awarded it, more than it deserves. But,

1. The opinions you have expressed are not peculiar opinions of your own, but common to you with a large class of Christian men, especially in the Northern States. They are, therefore, matters of public interest, and may properly be made the subject of public discussion.

2. Without any intention of controversy, either on your part or mine, the issues have fairly arisen between us in our published writings, for I have seldom seen the peculiar articles of Conservatism more distinctly and concisely presented than in your review. You give me credit for maintaining a "kind spirit," and for "fair-

---

* I use these terms not intending thereby to admit the propriety of their popular application, but, simply, because they are thus applied. Were I to designate the three parties, with an eye to the true nature and origin of their creeds, I should call them the *Philosophical*—using the word philosophy in the sense of what Paul designates as "science falsely so called" (1 Tim. 6 : 20), the *Philosophico-Scriptural* and the *Scriptural*. Whether such a designation would be a proper one, I submit to your judgment after you have read my letters.

ness," in writing on the subject of slavery. There is no need that I should "speak *your* praise" in the Presbyterian Church. As you truly say, " this delicate subject is growing in importance," and the discussion of it, in a Christian spirit, will do good, I believe, and not evil.

3. The points on which we differ lie entirely outside of the proper range of ecclesiastical action. Their discussion, therefore, cannot involve any "agitation" of the Church, though their decision in such a way that we all shall "see eye to eye"—if such a thing be possible—would greatly promote Christian sympathy among God's people, and advance the prosperity of Zion.

I heartily sympathize with you in the wish with which you close your article, that our Church shall not change "the scriptural position" which she has assumed on the subject of slavery. When she declared, in answer to certain memorials asking her to make slaveholding a subject of discipline, "Since Christ and his inspired Apostles did not make slaveholding a bar to communion, *we, as a court of Christ, have no authority to do so;* since they did not attempt to remove it from the Church by legislation, *we have no authority to legislate on the subject*" (see Digest, p. 813), she made a deliverance on slavery which covers all proper ground of ecclesiastical action, and a deliverance perfectly satisfactory, in so far as I know, to our whole Church at the South. This "scriptural position" has secured for her peace in the midst of abounding contention; and I can wish, "for Zion's sake," she may ever maintain that position.

Outside of the proper range of ecclesiastical action, however, there are points on which good men may honestly differ. Such are the points to which I propose directing your attention in the present letters.

1. We differ respecting the proper statement of the doctrine of scripture respecting slavery.

Your statement of that doctrine is,—" Slavery is not *necessarily and in all circumstances* sinful."—(*Pres. Mag.* p. 422.)

My statement of it is,—"Slaveholding is not a *sin* in the sight of God, and is not to be accounted an '*offence*' by his Church."—(*Chn. Doc. Slav.* p. 8.)

Taking your statement, in connection with your expressed wish that our Church should not change the position she has assumed on the subject of slavery, a fair interpretation of it must make it cover, in so far as ecclesiastical action is concerned, all that mine does. Yet, no one can read the two, when thus placed side by side, without feeling that they differ, at least in tone and spirit. And I now raise the question: *Which statement of the doctrine best accords with the teaching and spirit of the Word of God?*

That we may answer this question intelligently let us look at it,—

First, As a statement, in general terms, of a conclusion from admitted, scriptural, premises.

The statement of these premises in the "Christian Doctrine of

Slavery," pp. 102, 103, a statement to which you do not object, is in these terms: "In our examination of what the New Testament teaches on the subject of slavery, we have found, 1, That slave-holding does not appear in any catalogue of sins or 'offences' given us by inspired men; 2, That the Apostles received slaveholders into the Christian Church, and continued them therein, without giving any intimation, either at the time of their reception or after-wards, that slaveholding was a sin or an 'offence;' 3, That Paul sent back a fugitive slave to his own master again, and assigned as his reason for so doing, that master's right to the services of his slave; 4, That the Apostles frequently enjoin the relative duties of master and slave, and enforce their injunctions upon both alike, as Christian men, by Christian motives, uniformly teaching certain evils which they sought to correct, as incidental evils, and not 'part and parcel' of slavery itself; 5, That Paul treated the distinctions which slavery creates as matters of very little importance, in so far as the interests of the Christian life are concerned; 6, That he declares that this his doctrine respecting the relation of slave and master, is wholesome doctrine, and according to godliness, and the doctrine of the Lord Jesus Christ; 7, And directs Christian minis-ters to teach it in the Church, and prohibits the teaching of any doctrine at variance with it, under the most solemn sanctions known to the Church."

Such are the premises,—fairly stated. What is a proper state-ment, in general terms, of the logical conclusion therefrom? Is it simply, "Slavery is not *necessarily and in all circumstances* sin-ful?" Or, is it, "Slaveholding is not a sin in the sight of God, and is not to be accounted an 'offence' by his Church?"

Second, Let us look for a decision in a different direction, and ask, which statement best accords with the tone and spirit in which the scriptural deliverances on this subject are made?

And here, without examining each of the several passages which might be quoted, let us turn, at once, to that which of all others may most properly be appealed to, to decide the question, viz.: 1 Tim. 6 : 1–5. Here inspired Paul is giving instruction to Timo-thy, a minister of the Gospel, respecting what he should *teach*, and "how he ought to behave himself" in the Church of God. For this reason we are bound to consider this as the instruction of the One Head of the Church to the ministers of that Church respecting their duty as teachers and rulers in the Church, *i. e.*, it is express instruction to us on the very point we are examining.

"Let as many servants (*douloi*), as are under the yoke, count their own masters (*despotas*) worthy of all honour, that the name of God and his doctrine be not blasphemed. And they that have believing masters (*despotas*) let them not despise them because they are brethren; but rather do them service, because they are faithful and beloved partakers of the benefit. These things *teach and exhort.* If any man teach otherwise, and consent not to

wholesome words, even the words of our Lord Jesus Christ, and to
the doctrine which is according to godliness, he is proud, knowing
nothing, but doting about questions and strifes of words, whereof
cometh envy, strife, railings, evil surmisings, perverse disputings
of men of corrupt minds, and destitute of the truth, supposing that
gain is godliness,—*from such withdraw thyself.*"

Is there no discord to your ear between Paul's "certain sound,"
"wholesome words, even the words of our Lord Jesus Christ, and the
doctrine which is according to godliness," and such quavering notes
as "not necessarily" and in all "circumstances?" Or,—Take the
whole passage, read it over carefully, examine each of its several
clauses, try not simply to get at the truth it contains, but try to
catch the spirit of the passage ; and then, make a deliverance on
slavery, in general terms, and see if it will assume the form,—
"Slavery is not *necessarily and in all circumstances* a sin ;" or,
"Slaveholding is not a sin in the sight of God, and is not to be
accounted an 'offence' by his Church."

You may say, the two statements mean substantially the same
thing. Even granting that such is the intention of those who
use them, I object to your statement, because,—1. It is an unusual
form of stating ethical propositions such as this, and though it is
broad enough to acquit the slaveholding member of the Church, it
gives to his acquittal a sort of "whip, and clear him" air—pardon
my use of this homely expression : I can find no other which will
so well convey the exact idea I wish to give utterance to—which
seems to me, in contrast with all the New Testament deliverances
on the subject.

2. When taken apart from all explanations—and every general
proposition should be so expressed as to bear such examination—
it does not fairly cover all the ground which the doctrine of Christ
and his inspired Apostles covers.

I know—I think—your objections to such a statement of the
doctrine as I am contending for ; and, if I am right as to what
those objections are, a little impartial, ingenuous examination will
satisfy you that they are all groundless. You, probably, would
ask,—

1. Does not the statement "slaveholding is not a sin in the sight
of God, and is not to be accounted an 'offence' by his Church,"
involve the idea that all slaveholding is sinless in the sight of God?
I answer, by no means. When we affirm that marriage is not a
sin in the sight of God, we do not mean, nor are we understood to
affirm that all marriages are lawful—marriages contracted within
the "prohibited degrees," for example. As the proposition is one
based upon the law of God, the marriage to which alone it properly
applies, must subsist in accordance with the requirements of that
law. There is a slaveholding which the Word of God teaches us
is "consistent with Christian character and profession (that is,
consistent with justice, mercy, holiness, love to God and love to

man)." *Hodge.* The nature of this slaveholding, the law of God defines. When, then, we state the proposition that "slaveholding is not a sin in the sight of God," it can properly apply to such slaveholding only as subsists in conformity with the law of God.

2. Does not such a statement involve the idea of the perpetuity of slavery? I answer, by no means. When we affirm that despotic government in France, at the present day—demanded, as I believe, and I doubt not you do too, by the general good of the French nation—is not sinful in the sight of God; or, when we give utterance to a more general proposition, yet covering this particular case, and say, civil government is ordained of God; we do not mean to affirm, nor does any man understand us as affirming, the perpetuity of despotic government in that country. The time may come when the general good will demand a different form of government for France, and there is nothing in the general truth expressed in the proposition, "civil government is ordained of God," to forbid the French nation, when that time does come, taking measures to secure a different form of government for themselves, in any lawful way.

3. It is conceded, on all hands, that there are incidental evils attaching to slavery as it exists in this country, and in our day. Will not such a statement of the doctrine be so misunderstood by many, as to render them indifferent to the removal of those evils? Here, again, I answer by no means. And I answer thus confidently, because I feel that I have firm ground upon which to stand.

The Word of God is *the* standard in Christian ethics. Its deliverances are the result of a better than human wisdom,—better, not only as a superior wisdom, but as a wisdom guided and governed by perfect benevolence. If, then, the Word of God makes its deliverances in a certain way, I *know* that that is the best way—the way in which the truth will soonest and most certainly work out its appropriate result. Paul has written some things on the subject of slavery, which, judging from what we see throughout our land, "are hard to be understood, which they that are unlearned and unstable will wrest as they do also the other scriptures." (2 Pet. 3 : 16.) But of this we may rest assured. We will never mend the matter in this particular, by attempting to improve upon the deliverances of the Word of God.

GEO. D. ARMSTRONG.

LETTER II.

EMANCIPATION AND THE CHURCH.

To the Rev. C. Van Rensselaer: Having examined the question—What is a proper statement of the Scripture doctrine of slavery?—I will now ask your attention to another point on which we differ, viz. :

II. The proper *work* of the Church—the object and end which she is to keep in view in her labours for and with the slave race in our country. And let me ask you to especially note the fact, that it is the work of the *Church*, and not the work of the Christian citizen, in his character as a citizen, about which I raise a question.

On this point—

You write—"We regard the Christian instruction and elevation of the slaves as a means to an end, and that end is the recovery of the blessings of personal liberty, when Providence opens the way for it. The higher end is the salvation of their souls." (*Pres. Mag. p.* 422.)

I have written—"In the case of a race of men in slavery, the *work* which God has appointed his Church—as we learn it, both from the example and the precepts of inspired men—is to labour to secure in them a Christian life on earth and meetness for his heavenly kingdom." (*Chn. Doc. Sla. p.* 131.)

What you have set forth as "*the higher* end" of Christian instruction, is just what I hold to be *the one* end at which the Church is to aim. As to this end then we agree.

We differ in that you teach that the Church, in addition to this, should aim at securing for the slave—in your own language—"*the blessing of personal liberty, when Providence opens the way for it.*"

Before entering upon the examination of the point of real difference between us, I must strip your proposition of the adventitious support it derives from the terms in which you have expressed it. And I shall do this the more carefully, and, if possible, distinctly, because you have expressed it in the same terms in which I have often seen it expressed before; and, if I mistake not, it is mainly through the influence of this adventitious support it has found favour among good men.

1. On the phrase—"*the blessings of personal liberty*"—listen to Samuel Nott, whose "Slavery and the Remedy" you so highly commend. "Unhappily, this question of *well-being*, is kept out of sight amidst the earnest discussions of the times. Personal freedom is assumed as an absolute good, and in this 'petitio principii' the great question of practical well-being is altogether overlooked. Admit the evil to be such that no man can rightly reduce another man to slavery, any more than to poverty, sickness, or broken bones; admit that slavery as it is has more woes than belong to a merely servile condition, and demanding the speediest possible remedy; it does not follow hence, that the whole condition of the enslaved requires to be changed, without discrimination of the evil and the good. You must remove the evil, but you must not remove the good; you must remove the injurious and destructive, but you must not remove the beneficial and conservative. A Christian State, philanthropic and patriarchal, is bound to abolish just so much of slavery as it is, as is injurious, and no more; to retain just so much as is beneficial, and no less; seeking in very deed the well-being of the enslaved race, and that common good in which alone their welfare can be found." (pp. 24, 25.)

2. On the phrase—"*when Providence shall open the way for it*"—I remark, Providence never does "open the way"—in the sense in which you use that expression—for any change, unless well-being is to be promoted thereby. In writing, then, in terms which imply that Providence will open the way for the slave's recovering his personal freedom—for you write, "*when* Providence shall," and not *if* Providence shall—you are assuming a second time the controverted point, "that personal freedom is an absolute good."

Strip your proposition of this double *petitio principii*, and it will stand,—*We regard the Christian instruction of the slaves, as a means to an end, and that end is their emancipation before very long.*

Here I take issue with you. I affirm that ... question of the emancipation of the slave is one with which "Christian instruction," i. e. the instruction of the Church—for so the "higher end" you mention requires me to understand that phrase—has nothing directly to do. The Church has no right to set before herself such an end, as an end either higher or lower, of her labours.

You and I hold one opinion respecting the nature of the Church. The Church is no Voluntary Society, constituted by man, and therefore, liable to be modified and fashioned at his will. It is the kingdom of the Lord Jesus Christ. From him it derives its charter. His word is its law. By his instructions the Church is to abide, teaching all that he has commanded; and where he has given no command, placing her hand upon her lips.

On this matter of emancipation, Christ has given no command to his Church. The Word of God contains no deliverance, either express or clearly implied, respecting it. Hence, I affirm, the Church has no right to make a deliverance respecting it; much less, to set it before herself as an end of her labours. For an examination of 1 Cor. 7 : 21, "if thou mayest be made free, use it rather,"—I refer you to the " Chn. Doc. Slav.," especially the remarks on pp. 71–74.

The question of emancipation is a question concerning civil rights, and the relations of capital and labour, and is therefore essentially a political and not a religious question. And the Bible treats it just as it treats all other questions of the same kind,—it makes no deliverance on the subject, but leaves it to be determined by the State, in view of her responsibility to God for the well-being of the subject; the Church having no right to interfere.

So important does the observance of this distinction between the proper province of the Church and the State appear to me, especially at the present time, that I have discussed the subject at some length in the " Christian Doctrine of Slavery." Let me apply the principles there laid down to the two points in which we differ. Christ requires the Church to teach that the relations which slavery establishes are not sinful relations; and to teach the duties which grow out of those relations, to masters and slaves alike, and by her discipline to enforce the discharge of those duties, in so far as her members are concerned. Here her duty ceases. Does any member of the Church believe that slavery is a political evil ?—as a teacher and ruler in the Church, I have no difference with him. Does he teach this his faith, but teach it somewhere else than in the pulpit ?—I have no difference with him. Does he, availing himself of the rights which belong to a citizen in a republic, act and vote in accordance with this, his faith ?—I have no difference with him. And on the other hand, Does another believe that slavery is a political good, and teach and act upon this, his faith ?—I have no more difference with him than I had with the former. So with respect to emancipation. Does any Christian citizen believe that he ought to aim at the ultimate or even speedy emancipation of the slaves in our Southern States ?—I have no difference with him on this account. Does he teach and labour to carry into effect these his views, in a lawful way ?—I have no difference with him. And on the other hand, Does another believe that he ought to aim at the perpetuation of slavery, and teach and act upon this his faith, provided he does it lawfully ?—I have no difference with him therefor. These are all questions which lie outside the province of the Church. Anti-slavery and pro-slavery men, if the terms anti-slavery and pro-slavery be understood to refer to the question of expediency, or political good and evil, may all be alike worthy members of the Church. Differences on such points as these should no more interfere with their hearty co-operation in building up the kingdom of God in the world, than differences respecting the tariff, or the distribution of the public lands. But does any man, anti-slavery or pro-slavery, attempt to bring these matters into the Church, that he may get from the Church a decision, or enlist the Church in the cause he has espoused, I meet him at the threshold with the Master's command : "Render unto Cæsar the things that are Cæsar's," as well as "unto God the things that are God's." (Matt. 22 : 21.)

The commission Christ has given his Church, "Go ye into *all the world*, and preach the Gospel to *every creature*," requires her to preach that Gospel to the slave as well as the master. The inevitable effect, an effect which God designed, of this preaching, when faithfully done, must be the elevation of those to whom it is preached. But this truth no more necessarily implies the disappearance of slavery than it does the disappearance of poverty from among men. If, in time, the well-being of the slave—well-being in the highest and most comprehensive sense of that phrase—requires his emancipation, his emancipation will just as certainly take place as that God rules. And just as firmly as I believe this, do I believe, that when it comes, if come it does, as national independence came to our country, it will come without any violation of that order which God has established in the world; and hence, through the agency of the State, and not that of the Church.

You cannot be ignorant of the fact that the question of emancipation is a question surrounded with many difficulties—and let me add, difficulties which grow out of the obligation to provide for the well-being of the slave, far more than the master—and is a question upon which good and wise men honestly differ. Bishop Hopkins, of Vermont, for example, in his "American Citizen," a work which does credit alike to his head and his heart, contends for ultimate emancipation. Rev. Samuel Nott, of Massachusetts (and I purposely take cases from among the inhabitants of non-slaveholding States), of whom you speak as "a returned missionary, one of the earliest of the self-sacrificing band who went forth to the heathen," and who, hence, may fairly be presumed to be a godly man, and one practically acquainted with man in a degraded condition, on the other hand, in his "Slavery and the Remedy," takes opposite ground; and all his remedial suggestions are predicated upon the perpetuation of slavery in the Southern States. These men, no doubt, honestly differ ; and they have a right to differ here, without the Church calling either in question for his opinion.

You will now see clearly the grounds upon which I object to your opinion. They are :

1st. It determines what the Word of God leaves undetermined. In this it is *extra-scriptural.*

2d. It calls for uniformity of opinion where Christ allows liberty. In this it is *unscriptural.*

3d. It obtrudes the Church into the province which God has assigned to the State.   In this it is *anti-scriptural*.

You will see, too, why in the "Christian Doctrine of Slavery," you could find no expression of opinion on the subject of emancipation.   There was no expression of opinion there.   I expressly disclaimed the intention of treating slavery as a civil or political question.   That had been done by others far more ably than I could hope to do it; and I had nothing new to offer on the subject.   A brief and faithful exhibition of what Christ and his Apostles taught, *i. e.*, a discussion of slavery as a religious question, it seemed to me might do good ; and to this I pledged myself in the "Preface." The responsibility resting upon the preacher, in the pulpit, and the expositor of Scripture—whether his exposition be monographic or general—when writing for the press, is a very solemn responsibility.   His duty is clearly set forth in the words : "Son of man, I have made thee a watchman unto the house of Israel: therefore hear the word at my mouth, and give them warning from me." (Ezek. 3 : 17.)   The mixture of human opinions with God's truth has been one grand source of the evil which the Church has suffered in connection with this very matter ; of this, I shall take occasion to speak more fully in my last letter.

Your testimony—" On this point (*i. e.* emancipation) he is less explicit and full than we could desire.   Indeed, his cautious language in one paragraph indicates a timidity and uncertainty entirely uncalled for ; and some might even suppose that his views were either indifferent to emancipation, or even opposed to it.   This we do not believe ; but the paragraph reminds us of the doctrine of the Puseyites, who at times practise reserve in the communication of religious knowledge"—I was glad to receive : and I can well afford to pardon the lack of holiday dress in which the messenger presents himself, for the sake of the tidings which he brings.

In concluding this letter, let me say—Do not confound the cause of Liberian Colonization, with the question respecting the general, ultimate emancipation of the slaves in our Southern States.   The ground upon which our ablest Christians, philanthropists, and statesmen have advocated that cause would remain, even if it were determined that a general emancipation would never take place.

On this point, Bishop Hopkins has well written—" That a portion of the slaves will always be found worthy to be emancipated, as being possessed of more industry and talent than the average, is doubtless true, and such cases may safely be trusted to their master's liberality, or to the interest which they rarely fail to excite amongst others.   That there is another portion likely to be dissatisfied and refractory is also true, and the number of slaves who run away affords the evidence.   But there are exceptions to the general rule, about as numerous, perhaps, as the cases amongst the free labourers of other countries, where a few, possessed of extraordinary energy, are seen to rise up from a very low beginning, and another few prove worthy of the penitentiary; while the vast majority continue where they were, through the *slavery of circumstances*, which proves to be about as strong as any other kind of bondage, amongst the masses of mankind. For that portion who desire and are qualified for freedom, our Southern philanthropists have provided, of their own accord, the noble colony of Liberia, now advanced so far as to be an object of great interest among the nations." *American Citizen,* pp. 134, 135.

Here is ground upon which the Christian philanthropist who believes that the general emancipation of the slaves in our Southern States will never take place, may yet consistently advocate the cause of Liberia. And let me add—if we believe the testimony of such men as Dr. J. L. Wilson (see his "Western Africa"), and other judicious pious men who have been in Liberia—that colony is likely to receive accessions from this source alone, as large as she will be able to receive with safety to herself, for years to come: and no more disastrous event could occur to her, at the present time, than the landing upon her shore, not fifty but even five thousand emancipated slaves per annum, as has been proposed in some of the schemes of emancipation which find favour with good men, especially in the Northern States.

GEORGE D. ARMSTRONG.

LETTER III.

To the Rev. C. Van Rensselaer, D.D.: In my former letters I have examined the two articles which make up the peculiar creed of the conservative, as he is called. In the present, I will ask your attention to certain facts in the history of Anti-slavery opinions; and this, for the sake of the practical lesson which they teach.

Bishop Hopkins, in his "American Citizen," after briefly exhibiting the scriptural proof that slaveholding is not a sin, writes: "If we go on from the days of the Apostles to examine the doctrine and practice of the Christian Church, we find no other views entertained on the subject. Slavery continued to exist in every quarter. Slaves were held, without any reproach, even by the bishops and clergy. When the practice died out, as it did in many of the European nations, the change was gradual, through the operation of worldly causes, and without any suspicion that the institution, in itself, involved a violation of religion or morality. Hence its lawfulness with respect to the African and the Indians taken in war, was universally maintained by the Puritan settlers of New England, who claimed the closest adherence in all things to the teachings of the Scriptures. And it was not until the latter part of the eighteenth century that a doubt was expressed, on either side of the Atlantic, in relation to the perfect consistency of such slavery with the precepts of the Gospel."

"Since that time, indeed, public opinion, both in Old and New England, has undergone a great revolution. But this cannot be attributed to the Bible, nor to the Church, nor to any new knowledge of the will of God, nor to the discovery of any unknown principles of moral action. All that belongs to these was perfectly familiar to the Christian world from the days of the Apostles. And therefore no intelligent and candid mind can be surprised to find that the most violent opponents of slavery in the United States are always ready to wrest the Bible and denounce the Church, because they cannot derive from either the slightest real supports in their assaults against the lawfulness of the institution." (pp. 129, 130.)

The correctness of this brief history of the progress of Anti-slavery opinions, no one, I presume, will seriously question. And the point to which I would, now, particularly call your attention, is that presented in the words—" *it*," i. e., this change, " *cannot be attributed to the Bible, nor to the Church.*" It was not from the Bible these opinions originated; it was not in the Church they first saw the light.

Whence are they? I answer: They can be distinctly traced back to their origin in that infidel philosophy on the subjects of civil government and human liberty, which, becoming popular in the latter half of the last century, had its culmination, in the one direction, in the French revolution, and in the other, in the disastrous emancipation effected in the British West India Islands: a philosophy which substitutes for the Bible account of the origin of civil government in the family, the theory of the " civil compact," as it has been called; and confounds human liberty with unbridled license.

You are familiar with the classic story of the fall of Troy;—how, concealed in a wooden horse, consecrated to Diana, the enemy found admission into that doomed city. In a way very similar has this infidel philosophy found admission into the Church of God. Of the mischief it has already wrought there, in rending the Church, in making enemies of those who should be friends, in prostituting the pulpit and desecrating the Sabbath by substituting the preaching of politics in the place of the Gospel, there is no need that I should tell you.

This heresy—for surely, I do it no wrong when I apply to it the name of heresy—has made its most insidious approaches, and gained its most dangerous advantages, by subtly mingling its errors with God's truths, in our popular expositions of Scripture. As it is here, in the permanent printed page, its progress can be traced with least danger of falling into error, let me ask you to compare the exposition of a passage of Scripture bearing on the subject of slavery, written before this infidel philosophy, " this science, falsely so called" obtained currency, with one written after it had begun to prevail, and another written in this, our day.

Let us take a part of the passage to which attention has been already turned in my first letter, viz., 1 Tim. 6 : 2, " And they that have believing masters, let them not despise them, because they are brethren; but rather do them service, because they are faithful and beloved, partakers of the benefit. These things teach and exhort."

Turn now to Matthew Henry's Exposition, written early in the last century, and you will read: " Or suppose the master were a Christian and a believer, and the servant a believer too; would not that excuse him, because *in Christ there is neither bond nor free?*

No, by no means, for Jesus Christ did not come to dissolve the bond of civil relation, but to strengthen it: *They that have believing masters, let them not despise them, because they are brethren;* for that brotherhood relates only to spiritual privileges, not to any outward dignity or advantage (those misunderstand and abuse their religion, who make it a pretence for denying the duties that they owe to their relations); nay, *rather do them service, because they are faithful and beloved.* They must think themselves the more obliged to serve them, because the faith and love which bespeak men Christians, oblige them to do good; and that is all wherein their service consists. Observe, It is a great encouragement to us in doing our duty to our relations, if we have reason to think they are faithful and beloved, *and partakers of the benefit,* that is, of the benefit of Christianity. Again, Believing masters and servants are brethren, and partakers of the benefit; for in Christ Jesus there is neither bond nor free, for ye are all one in Christ Jesus. (Gal. 3 : 28.) Timothy is appointed *to teach and exhort these things.* Ministers must preach, not only the general duties of all, but the duties of particular relations.''

Here, all is plain, straightforward exposition of the text. The author evidently writes with a " single eye" to the exhibition of " the truth, the whole truth, and nothing but the truth'' contained in the passage of Scripture he is expounding.

Dr. Thomas Scott wrote his Commentary about the close of the last century; the first edition was published in 1796. Let us look, now, at his exposition of this passage; and, I select the Commentary of Scott, because the unquestioned piety of the man, and the general excellence of his work, render the peculiarity to which I would direct attention, all the more conspicuous.

"And such of them," *i. e.,* 'servants,' as enjoy the privilege of 'believing masters,' ought by no means to despise them, or withhold from them due respect and obedience; because they were brethren in Christ, and so upon a level in respect of religious privileges; but rather 'to do them service' with double diligence and cheerfulness, because of their faith in Christ, and their interest in his love, as partakers of the inestimable benefit of his salvation. This shows that Christian masters were not required to set their slaves at liberty.''

Thus far, all is plain, straightforward exposition of what Paul has written. If any man will gainsay it, his controversy is not with Dr. Scott, the expositor, but with inspired Paul, the author. But Scott adds, " though they were instructed to behave towards them in such a manner as would *greatly lessen* and *nearly annihilate* the evils of slavery.'' Here the influence of this false philosophy begins to appear;—and I object to this statement, not simply on the ground that it is not in the text, but mainly, because it is a partial statement of truth, and thus, practical error. Paul never uses such paltering terms as " greatly lessen'' and

" nearly annihilate," when dealing with the master respecting his
" behaviour" toward his slaves. That we may see how Paul does
deal with this subject, turn to Col. 6 : 1, and read—" Masters,
give unto your servants that which is just and equal ; knowing
that ye also have a Master in heaven." See also Eph. 6 : 9.
Paul is here enjoining their relative duties upon *masters* and servants, along with husbands and wives, parents and children, and
he enjoins these duties upon all alike, as Christians, by Christian
motives. But he knows well that the natural affections do not
afford as efficient protection to the slave as they do to the wife and
the child, and hence—when he comes to deal with the master, he
cites him at once before our common " Master in heaven," and in
that awful presence he charges him, in view of the solemnities of
the judgment—" give unto your servants that which is just and
equal"—ALL, "that is just and equal." Now let this Christian
master go back to his house or plantation again, and he will not
be satisfied to " greatly alleviate," or " nearly annihilate" any evil
which concerns his " behaviour" to his servants ; he will seek to
remove it altogether.

Scott adds, yet further—"It would have excited much confusion,
awakened the jealousy of the civil powers, and greatly retarded
the progress of Christianity, had the liberation of slaves by their
converts been expressly required by the Apostles : though the
principles of both the law and the Gospel, when carried to their
consequences, will infallibly abolish slavery." Here, this philosophy shows itself more distinctly. There is nothing of all this in
the text. Taking the most favourable view of the case for the expositor, we say—It is not Paul's *truth*, it is Dr. Scott's *opinion*.
And yet, appearing where it does, most readers will take it all as
if it were the teaching of Scripture.

And it places the teaching of Christ and his Apostles on the
subject of slavery altogether in a wrong light. The amount of
this apology which Scott offers for this conduct, is well stated by
Dr. Hodge (see his " Essays and Reviews," pp. 488, 489), in the
words—" It amounts to this. Christ and his Apostles thought
slaveholding a great crime, but they abstained from saying so for
fear of the consequences. The very statement of the argument,
in its naked form, is its refutation." Thus has the Commentary of
so excellent a man as Dr. Scott been, here, " spoiled through his
philosophy." (Col. 2 : 8.)

Turn we now to an Exposition written in our day, when this
philosophy has "run to seed ;" the " Notes on the New Testament," by Rev. A. Barnes ; and that I may do him no injustice,
I shall give so much of his "Notes" as I quote, just as I find them
printed, italics, punctuation, and all. My edition is that of the
Harpers, 1853.

" 2. *And they that have believing masters.* Masters who are
Christians. It is clear from this, that Paul supposed that, at that

time, and under those circumstances, a man might *become* a Christian who had slaves under him. How long he might *continue* to hold his fellow men in bondage, and yet be a Christian, is, however, quite a different question."

Dr. Barnes's "*at that time, and in those circumstances,*" is a bowshot beyond Dr. Scott's "greatly alleviate and nearly annihilate," and yet there is a family likeness between them, that strikes you at a glance.

"*And yet be a Christian.*" Had Dr. Barnes been a professed Arminian, I should have understood him here, as referring to a threatening probability of "falling from grace:" but, as he claims to be a Calvinist, I see not how I can fairly interpret his language, unless I understand that these Christian slaveholders were only a sort of *quasi* Christians, after all; admitted into "the kingdom of God" in some such way as "mourners" are admitted into the Methodist Church—*on probation*—and not to be allowed to continue there unless they shortly renounced their slaveholding. Perhaps Dr. Barnes would say—such *quasi* Christians would answer "at that time and under those circumstances"—and certainly, all will agree with him, that this might just as well be, as that Christians should come into that kingdom at all, holding on to a sin worse than "piracy and murder."

"*Because they are faithful,* that is *because* they are *believers* or are Christians—*pistoi;* the same word which in the beginning of the verse is rendered *believing.* It does not here mean, that they were faithful to their servants or their God, but merely that they were Christians."

A strange sort of Christians these Ephesians must have been, who were not "*faithful*" to, *i. e.,* "*believers*" in—for so Dr. Barnes interprets the word faithful as used by Paul; and his marking it here with quotation marks, requires us to understand him as taking it from Paul's writing—their servants or their God. I do not know that I get exactly Dr. Barnes's idea—but a man who did not "believe in servants, or in God," I should call an Abolition atheist. Now, if these Ephesians, while they were slaveholders, were at heart Abolition atheists—the wonder is, not that they could enter the "kingdom of God" on no better terms than *probationers,* but that they could enter that kingdom at all.

But, enough—though there are some eight pages of these Notes on this passage in 1 Tim., over which one might well make merry, were it not so sad a thing to see the Word of God thus handled.

What is the principle which lies at the foundation of all such exposition of Scripture as this?—I will give it you in the very words of the Expositor himself: "I believe that there are great principles in our nature, as God has made us; which can never be set aside by any authority of a pretended revelation; and that if a book professing to be a revelation from God, by any fair interpretation defended slavery, or placed it on the same basis as the relation of husband and wife, parent and child, guardian and ward, such a book neither ought to be, nor could be received by mankind as a divine revelation." (Barnes's " Church and Slavery," p. 193.) And such notes as those I have quoted are the ravings of a man " doting" (*noson*, sick), 1 Tim. 6 : 4, from feeding on this philosophy, and in his delirium, sitting down to tinker the word of God, as wiser and holier than He.

In commenting on Paul's expression " wholesome words," Matthew Henry makes this weighty remark : " We observe (1), The words of our Lord Jesus Christ are wholesome words ; they are the fittest to prevent or heal the Church's wounds, as well as to heal a wounded conscience : for Christ has the tongue of the learned, to speak a word in season to him that is weary. (Isa. 1 : 4.) The words of Christ are the best to prevent ruptures in the Church ; for none who profess faith in him, will dispute the aptness or authority of his words, who is their Lord and teacher ; *and it has never gone well with the Church, since the words of men have claimed a regard equal to his words, and in some cases a much greater.*" That last clause may have been *prophecy*, when Henry wrote it ; it is *history* now.

Near the close of your article you write : " We believe that one of the providential calls on the Old School Presbyterian Church is *to stand in the gap*—to oppose unscriptural and fanatical extravagance in the North and in the South, in the East and in the West. Being on scriptural ground, we must not recede from it, either from fear of abolition clamour on the one hand or of slavery propagandism on the other." That is a noble Christian utterance. Let us thank God that the " old blue banner" does float " in the gap ;" for though there may be many a time-honoured standard in the field, there is none fitter to float " in the gap" than that which bears as its escutcheon " Christ's crown."

" CHRIST'S CROWN." Methinks the host marshalled under such a banner should have loyal hearts, and willingly submit themselves, in all things, to his rule : fighting just where he has placed them, and just as he has given them orders, trying to catch his spirit, ever watching his eye.

GEORGE D. ARMSTRONG.

DR. VAN RENSSELAER'S

THREE REPLIES

TO

DR. ARMSTRONG,

ON

THE SUBJECT OF SLAVERY.

THREE CONSERVATIVE REPLIES.

REPLY I.

ON THE PROPER STATEMENT OF THE SCRIPTURE DOCTRINE OF SLAVERY.

To THE REV. GEORGE D. ARMSTRONG, D.D.: Your three Letters on Slavery have been read by me with great interest. They cover ground, not often distinctly included in the field of discussion, and they exhibit diversities of sentiment which rightly claim a candid consideration.

The appellation of a "Conservative," which you have been pleased to apply to me, gives me satisfaction. I have always professed to be "conservative" on this exciting subject; repudiating, on the one hand, the fundamental principle of fanatical abolitionism, which makes slaveholding always and everywhere sinful, and, on the other hand, rejecting with equal conscientiousness the ultra defences of slavery, which constitute it a Divine ordinance, in the sense that civil government is "ordained of God," and which claim for it an undefined permanence.*

I follow your example in making a few preliminary remarks.

1. Some of our mutual friends, who are fearful of the agitation of slavery in our Church, have advised me not to reply to your letters. But if any danger was to be apprehended, the alarm ought to have been sounded before so much had been written from the other side of the line. It is quite probable that a brief notice of my brief review would have been allowed to pass without any answer. My position, however, is very much changed, after three long letters, containing an elaborate and skilful attack on the conservative views prevalent in the Presbyterian Church, have been extensively circulated. I am glad that you concur with me in the opinion that a discussion of the points at issue between us "cannot involve any agitation of the Church."

---

* I am a little surprised that, in the popular classification of "Abolitionist, Conservative, and Pro-slavery man," you so quietly assume the appellation of the latter. Whether I admit the propriety of your proposed designation of "Philosophical, Philosophico-Scriptural, and Scriptural," you will better understand after you have read my letters. The only true division is Scriptural and Unscriptural.

2. The whole truth pertaining to this subject, is of the utmost consequence. Slavery is among the prominent practical questions of the age. The destiny of several millions of human beings is more or less affected by the views of ministers and others, who, like yourself, possess an extensive influence in the formation of public opinion. I cannot shrink from any lawful responsibility in candidly and boldly maintaining what I conceive to be the true philosophy and morals of slavery, as set forth in the Scriptures, and in the testimonies of the Presbyterian Church. No servant of Christ should exhibit a false timidity, when providentially challenged to defend the right.

3. Your candour and courtesy are models for my imitation. We undoubtedly entertain sentiments in regard to slavery, coincident in the main, but varying in importance according to the standpoint of different readers. Neither of us is a prejudiced partisan. Like yourself, although born at the North, I have lived at the South, and have learned, both there and here, to sympathize with my brethren who are involved in the evils of this perplexing social system. In Virginia I completed my theological education, was licensed and ordained by " the laying on of the hands of the Presbytery" of West Hanover, and commenced my ministry as a missionary to the slaves, on the plantations of the Roanoke and Dan Rivers. These personalities are mentioned to show that we are, in some respects at least, on a level in this discussion. It is better for ministers of the same Church, who mutually appreciate each other's objects and position, and who endeavour candidly to arrive at the truth, to hold a Christian correspondence on slavery, than for boisterous and uncharitable partisans to break lances for victory in a crowd of excited spectators. The present opportunity is a good one for mutual explanations, which may possibly produce a nearer approximation to agreement than is indicated by the line of separation marked out by some of your arguments.

4. The discussion embraces the whole subject of slavery, and not merely the points which might by some be placed within the limits of Church authority. According to your judgment, " the points on which we differ, lie *entirely outside* of the proper range of ecclesiastical action." I shall hereafter express my views in regard to this particular opinion, contenting myself, for the present, with the simple affirmation, that I write with all the light I can obtain from the Bible, and with whatever illumination the Spirit of God may graciously grant. Without discussing at present the precise range of ecclesiastical action, I shall endeavour to seek " the truth, the whole truth, and nothing but the truth."

5. The general form of a discussion depends upon the positions of those who engage in it. When I discussed the subject of slavery in 1835, my object was to examine and expose the two fundamental principles of ultra abolitionism, viz., that slaveholding is always and everywhere sinful, and that emancipation is an immediate and

universal duty. On the present occasion I am called upon to defend the scriptural doctrine against arguments, which seem to advocate (in a comparatively mild form) ultra pro-slavery views. The Bible, as well as the Presbyterian testimony founded upon it, points to a clear, deep channel between these two dangerous passes. The Assembly's testimonies of 1818 and 1845, I regard as scriptural, harmonious, and, for the present at least, sufficient, occupying as they do, the true position between two extremes, and vindicating the opinions of those whom you rightly call "conservatives."

I now proceed to the subject of your first Letter, viz., THE PROPER STATEMENT OF THE SCRIPTURAL DOCTRINE OF SLAVERY.

Your statement is, "*Slaveholding is not a sin in the sight of God, and is not to be accounted an offence by his Church.*"

My statement is, "*Slaveholding* is not necessarily and in all circumstances sinful.*"

My statement was written *currente calamo*, without any intention to propound an exact formula of the scriptural doctrine. Some might prefer to either statement one in these words : "Slaveholding, in itself considered, is not sinful," or "All slaveholding is not sinful;" or "There is a slaveholding, which is consistent with the Christian profession." I adhere, however, to what I have written ; because, whilst my original form of statement includes the lawfulness of the relation, in itself considered, it also more clearly expresses the idea that circumstances may render the continuance of the relation wrong. It brings out, in my judgment, *more* scriptural truth on the subject than any of the forms mentioned, and especially than yours.

All admit that slavery, in a worse form than that which now exists in this country, prevailed throughout the Roman empire. As a *system* in actual operation, with its cruel laws and usages, the Apostles could have no more approved it than they did the despotism of Nero. And yet they nowhere condemned the relation itself as necessarily sinful. Despotism maintains a relation to civil government analogous to that which slaveholding sustains to the household. Absolute authority may exist in both relations, under certain circumstances, without sin. The inspired writers uniformly treat both despotism and slaveholding as forms of society which circumstances might justify.

The Bible contains no formal statement of the doctrine of slavery, but enforces the duties growing out of the relation. A correct statement of the scriptural mode of treating slavery might be in these words : "All masters and all slaves are bound to perform their relative duties, arising from legal authority on the one hand, and from enjoined submission on the other." You had, undoubtedly, the right to exhibit the doctrine of slaveholding in the more

---

* I have substituted "slaveholding" for "slavery," in order to remove all ambiguity in the terms.

abstract form, propounded in your volume. But, I think that the reader of your volume and letters does not receive the full impression of scripture truth and exhortation, properly pertaining to this subject. Your unqualified statement that "slaveholding is not a sin in the sight of God," seems to me to fall short of a perfect formula, even from "the admitted, scriptural premises" adduced, and by me cordially acquiesced in. I submit a brief commentary on these "admitted, scriptural premises," by way of developing the argument. 1. If "slaveholding does not appear in any catalogue of sins," this fact proves that it is not *malum in se.* It is also deserving of notice that slaveholding does not appear in any enumeration of virtues and graces. 2. The Apostles received slaveholders to the communion, and so they did despots and their abettors in Cæsar's household. 3. Paul sent back a fugitive slave, and would also have sent back a deserter from the imperial army. 4. The injunction to slaves to obey their masters does not approve of slavery, any more than the command to submit to "the powers that be," implied approbation of Nero's despotism. 5. The distinctions of slavery in regard to the interests of Christian life are, like all other outward distinctions, of comparatively little importance; and yet the general injunction of Paul on this subject was, " Art thou called, being a slave? care not for it. But if thou mayst be free, *use it rather.*" 6. The Christian doctrine of Paul respecting the mutual duties of masters and servants is clearly wholesome, and utterly subversive of modern abolitionism; but whilst it proves that the relation is not in itself sinful, it does not sanction the relation as a desirable and permanent one. 7. Christian ministers, who preach to the slaves insurrection, instead of submission, and who denounce slaveholding as necessarily and always sinful, are on unscriptural and dangerous ground.

In my judgment, your "admitted scriptural premises" do not warrant the unqualified statement of doctrine which you have laid down. My commentary is simply designed as a rebutter to your too broad conclusions.

Slaveholding, in itself considered, is not sinful; that is to say, it is not a *malum in se;* or, in other words, it is a relation that may be justified by circumstances. When we say that the relation itself is not sinful, we do not mean, by the expression, a mere abstraction; for slavery cannot be conceived of apart from a master and a slave. But we mean that slaveholding, as a practical relation, depends upon certain conditions for its justification. What is *malum in se* cannot be justified by any circumstances; the law of God always condemns it. But slaveholding being among things " *indifferent"* in morals, it may be right or wrong, according to the conditions of its existence. Hence your definition, which excludes circumstances, comes short of the full Scripture doctrine.

Three sources of your defective statement, as it appears to me, deserve consideration.

1st. You have erred in placing the relation of master and slave on the same basis with that of parent and child. Your illustration assumes too much on this point. There are specific and fundamental differences between these two relations. The marriage relation is divinely constituted; it existed anterior to sin; it is normal in its character and permanent in duration; and it is honourable in all. Whereas the relation of master and slave cannot be said to be more than providentially permitted or sanctioned; it originated as you admit, by the wickedness of "manstealing," and by a violation of the laws of God; it implies an abnormal condition of things, and is therefore temporary; and it must be acknowledged, that it is in discredit generally throughout Christendom. The two relations are quite distinct in their nature. That of master and slave is not, indeed, in itself sinful; but it cannot be looked upon with the complacency with which the parental relation is contemplated. The parental relation and slaveholding possess, of course, some affinities. They may fall into the same category, if the classification be made wide enough, for both belong to the social state and have relative duties. Or, if the classification be made even narrower, they may still be arranged under the same category, for both imply the possession of absolute power. But, if the classification be into natural relations, and those relations which arise from circumstances, then marriage goes into the former category, and slavery into the latter. It is only within a certain compass, therefore, that we can reason from one to the other, without danger of pernicious fallacies.

2. In the second place, your unqualified proposition that "slaveholding is not sinful," mistakes the scriptural view by implying its lawfulness *everywhere and under all circumstances.* The relation of master and slave may be lawful in Virginia at the present time. But is it lawful in New Jersey, or in New England? And will it *always* be lawful in Virginia? I apprehend not. The good of the slave and of the community is the great law controlling the existence of the relation. If a slaveholder were to remove from Virginia into New Jersey, your proposition loses all its virtue, and collapses into error. Slaveholding is sinful by the laws of that State; and even if there were no law prohibiting its existence on the statute-book, could the citizens of New Jersey become slaveholders under the plea that "slaveholding is not a sin in the sight of God?" Again, is it clear, that citizens in the Free States can always lawfully enter into this relation, when they remove into States where the laws sanction it? Under the shelter of your proposition, they might do so; but it is certain, that there are tens of thousands of Christians in the Free States, who could not enter voluntarily into this relation without involving their consciences in sin. Slavery, even in the Slave States, where it may lawfully exist at the present time, is abnormal and exceptional, and is to be justified only by circumstances. This your definition overlooks.

3. In the third place, your statement passes by the testimony of the Old Testament dispensation. Moses found slavery an institution in existence, and treated it as an admitted evil. Tolerating it under the peculiar condition of society, the laws of the Hebrew Commonwealth were framed with a view to mitigate its evils, to restrict its limits, and, finally, to discountenance it altogether. The distinction between the lawfulness of enslaving Israelites and Gentiles, with various other discriminating regulations, shows, that Moses took into view circumstances in his legislation on this subject. Even under the Jewish dispensation, your statements would not have been received as a full and definite exposition of the true doctrine of slavery. My original statement that " slaveholding is not necessarily and under all circumstances sinful," accords better, both with the letter of the Old Testament dispensation and the spirit of the New, than does yours.

What I especially insist upon, in a scriptural statement of the doctrine of slavery is, that the relation itself shall not be confounded with the injustice of slave laws on the one hand, nor separated, on the other hand, from the providential circumstances or condition of society, where it claims a lawful existence.

If you, therefore, ask, generally, why in my statement, I qualify the relation by the words "not necessarily and in all circumstances sinful," I reply, that the possession of despotic power is a thing to be justified, and for which a good reason is always to be given. Marriage is to continue as long as the race, and is in its own nature everywhere lawful. Not so with slavery. You, yourself, contend in your book, that it was originally wrong, and that the menstealers in Africa, and, inferentially, the slave-buyers in America, of that generation, sinned against God by their mutual traffic in flesh and blood. Slavery does not, like marriage, arise from the nature of man. It exists only from the peculiar condition of the slave class. And, therefore, a scriptural statement must not ignore a reference to providential developments ; and it is right to characterize the relation by words which qualify its lawfulness.

Again. If you ask how circumstances can make a relation sinful, which in itself may be lawful, I reply, that circumstances always control the moral character of those relations and actions, which belong in morals to things " indifferent," or *adiaphora.* Some things, like idolatry and manstealing, are *mala in se*, and can be justified by no circumstances whatever. Other things, like polygamy, were tolerated under the Old Testament dispensation, but not under the New. Other things, as slavery, were tolerated under both dispensations ; but neither under the Old nor the New dispensation was slavery recognized as lawful, apart from the circumstances of its origin and the attending conditions. The circumstances in the midst of which slaveholding finds itself, will always be an element to enter into its justification, or condemnation, at the bar of righteousness.

Again. If you press me still closer, and ask more particularly, how the qualifying and restrictive language employed by me, is consistent with the language of Scripture in regard to the duties of masters and slaves,—which many interpret as giving full and universal sanction to the system of slaveholding,—I reply, *first*, that the mere injunction of relative duties, as has been already intimated, does not imply full approbation of a relation, which circumstances may for a time render lawful, and the duties of which require clear specification. The general duty of submission to the established government, does not prove that all despots are sinless in obtaining and in retaining their absolute power. Servants are required to be subject not only to good and gentle, but to froward masters, who make them suffer wrongfully. (1 Peter 2 : 18, 19.) This, however, does not make such frowardness and cruelty, on the part of the masters, sinless. And, generally, the meekness with which we are required to bear insult and injury, does not justify those wrongs. Doddridge says, "I should think it unlawful to resist the most unjust power that could be imagined, if there was a probability of doing mischief by it." But this cannot make what is wrong and pernicious in any particular form or circumstances, sacred, divine, and immutable. Polygamy, which was tolerated under the Old Testament, under certain conditions, was a relation of mutual rights and obligations; but was polygamy, therefore, on a level with the marriage relation, and was it an institution that could be perpetuated without sin? Certainly not. Nor does the exhortation to masters and servants imply anything more than that the prescribed relative duties are to be discharged as long as the relation may be lawfully continued. *Secondly*, the duties of submission, heart-service, &c., on the part of the slaves, and the corresponding duties of the masters, belong to my statement as much as they do to yours. The performance of these mutual duties is essential to the solution of the problem of slavery, and to the inauguration of the new circumstances which may make its continuance a wrong. *Thirdly*, slaveholding not being a *malum in se*, no scriptural exhortation against the relation under all circumstances, would have been consistent with truth and righteousness. Hence, neither despotism nor slaveholding receives from the Scriptures the undiscriminating anathemas hurled by modern fanatics. Their temporary justification depends on circumstances of which the rulers and masters of each generation must judge, as in sight of the Ruler and Master in heaven. *Fourthly*, The general spirit of the doctrines and precepts of the Bible operates unequivocally and decidedly against the permanence of slavery in the household, or of despotism in the state. An emphatic testimony is rendered on the pages of revelation against these relations, whose origin is in human sins and woes, and whose continuance is justified only by the public good. Instead of precise rules, which the wisdom of God has not prescribed for the eradication of all the evils of society, the Gospel substitutes sublime and heart-moving principles, which make the Christian " a law unto himself," and transform, through the Spirit, human nature into the image of the divine.

After all, we both agree in the fundamental position that slavery *may* exist without sin; that the relation, in itself considered, is not sinful. You prefer your statement of the doctrine, and I prefer mine. You imagine, in comparing my statement with Scripture, that you discern "discord," and catch the sound of "quavering notes;" whilst, to my ears, your statement sounds like an old tune with unpleasant alterations, and withal, set on so high a key as to endanger falsetto in unskilful voices. It is my honest conviction that my formula approaches the nearest to the true doctrine of Scripture.

The correctness of my form of statement is, I think, confirmed by several considerations.

In the first place, this mode of stating the scriptural doctrine of slavery *coincides with the testimonies of the Presbyterian Church.* The General Assembly of 1818 uses the following language:

" We do, indeed, tenderly sympathize with those portions of our Church and our country where the evil of slavery has been entailed; where a great, and the most virtuous, part of the community abhor slavery, and wish its extermination as sincerely as any others; but where the number of slaves, their ignorance, and their vicious habits generally, render an immediate and universal emancipation *inconsistent alike with the safety and happiness of the master and slave.* With those who are *thus circumstanced,* we repeat that we tenderly sympathize. At the same time, we earnestly exhort them to continue, and, if possible, to increase their exertions to effect a total abolition of slavery. We exhort them to suffer no greater delay to take place in this most interesting concern, than *a regard to the public welfare* truly and indispensably demands."

Here, it will be seen, the doctrine of our Assembly is, that circumstances control the continuance of slavery. This relation is justifiable, or otherwise, according as "the happiness of the master and slave" and "the public welfare" are promoted by it.

The paper adopted by the General Assembly in 1845, by a vote of 168 to 13, assumes the same principle, and substantially adopts the form of my original statement. It says:

"The question, which is now unhappily agitating and dividing other branches of the Church, is whether the holding of slaves is, *under all circumstances,* a heinous sin, calling for the discipline of the Church." p. 812. "The question, which this Assembly is called upon to decide is this : Do the Scriptures teach that the holding of slaves, *without regard to circumstances*, is a sin ?" p. 812.

You perceive that the question is stated in words which resemble very much the words of a " Conservative." Further :

" The Apostles did not denounce the *relation itself* as sinful." "The Assembly cannot denounce the holding of slaves as *necessarily* a heinous and scandalous sin." p. 812. "The existence of domestic slavery, *under the circumstances* in which it is found in the southern portion of the country, is no bar to Christian communion." p. 813.

Whilst my statement of the doctrine of slavery coincides with the utterances of the Church, many will think that yours comes far short of it. Whatever added explanations may cause it to approximate to the language of the General Assembly, the naked words are as dissimilar, as a leafless tree is from one of living green.

As you frequently quote Dr. Hodge, I also will take the liberty of exhibiting the opinions of the distinguished Professor, in their true connection with the point at issue. I ask your particular attention to these extracts from the Biblical Repertory, which might be extended, if necessary.

" An equally obvious deduction [from the Scriptures] is, that slave-holding is *not necessarily sinful.*" 1836, p. 277.

" Both political despotism and domestic slavery belong in morals to the *adiaphora*, to things indifferent. They may be expedient or inexpe-dient, right or wrong, *according to circumstances*. Belonging to the same class, they should be treated in the same way. Neither is to be denounced as *necessarily sinful*, and to be abolished immediately *under all circum-stances.*" p. 286.

" Slavery is a question of circumstances, and not a *malum in se.*" " Simply to prove that slaveholding interferes with natural rights, is not enough to justify the conclusion that it is *necessarily* and universally *sin-ful.*" p. 292.

" These forms of society [despotism, slavery, &c.] are not necessarily, or in themselves, just or unjust ; but become one or the other *according to circumstances.*" p. 295.

" Monarchy, aristocracy, democracy, domestic slavery, are right or wrong, as they are, *for the time being, conducive to this great end* [intel-lectual and moral elevation] or the reverse." p. 302.

" We have ever maintained that slaveholding is *not in itself sinful; that the right to personal liberty is *conditioned* by the ability to exercise bene-ficially that right.*" 1849, p. 601.

" Nothing can be more distinct than the right to hold slaves *in certain circumstances*, and the right to render slavery perpetual." p. 603.

These quotations prove that Dr. Hodge unites with the great body of our Church, north and south, east and west, in limiting the lawfulness of slaveholding by the very terms of its formal defi-

nition, at the same time that he earnestly contends, with all who
are on scriptural ground, that the relation, in itself considered, is
not sinful. The "conservatives" of the Church everywhere uphold
all the testimonies of the General Assembly in their true sprit and
very letter.

Another consideration, confirming the belief that my statement
is the better of the two, is that *it is more philosophical in its form.*
The conditions of an ethical proposition relating to slavery, as
furnished by yourself, are threefold. 1. The proposition must be
in the usual form of ethical propositions. 2. It must be so expressed as to require no explanations. 3. It should cover all the
ground which Christianity covers.

1. The usual form of ethical propositions in regard to *adiaphora*, or things indifferent, includes a reference to circumstances.
Whether the proposition be expressed in a positive or negative form,
is not of much account, provided the meaning be clear. Your own
statement is a negative one ; but the difficulty is that its meaning
is not plain. If the word *despotism*, or *war*, be substituted for
slavery in our respective statements, I think you will see at once
that your statement does not express the true idea, so well as mine.
The proposition that " despotism, or war, is not a sin in the sight
of God," is not a true ethical proposition. Because, like slavery,
despotism and war seek their justification in circumstances. Circumstances cannot be omitted from a philosophical proposition on
" things indifferent."

Your objection to my statement appears to be that it does not
clearly admit the morality of slaveholding, but that it acquits the
master with a sort of " whip, and clear him" judgment. This latter
expression, if I understand it, means " strike first, and then acquit."
Very far from such a rude proceeding is the intention, or tendency,
of my argument. The force of it is simply to put the slaveholder
in a position which demands him to justify himself before God,
which every Christian ought always to be ready to do. I explicitly
maintain that the relation may be a lawful one, and that the Christian performance of its duties often brings peculiar honour upon
the slaveholder, and calls into exercise some of the most shining
graces of the Gospel. But slaveholding, although not *malum in se*,
is not a natural and permanent phase of civilization. Like despotism or war, it is to be justified, or condemned, by the condition of
things and the necessities of the case. It does not, in itself, imply
an unchristian spirit, or unchristian conduct ; and hence our Church
has always refused to recognize it as under all circumstances an
" offence" and " a bar to Christian communion." My proposition
throws no suspicion, or reproach, upon any one who is in a true
and justifiable position ; and the very fact that it includes circumstances as an element in the solution of its morality, proves it to be
philosophically sound.

2. If the proposition, in order to be correctly stated, must require no explanations, I think that my form has considerable advantage over yours. "Slavery is not necessarily and in all circumstances sinful" is a general proposition, containing, without the need of explanation, the ethical truths on the subject. Your proposition, "Slavery is not a sin in the sight of God," is liable at once to the doubt, whether it is intended to be a universal or a particular proposition ; that is, whether you mean to say, "*no* slaveholding is sinful," or only that "*some* slaveholding is not sinful." The needed explanation, against which you protest, is actually given by you in another part of your letter, where you say that your statement by no means "involves the idea that all slaveholding is sinless in the sight of God," or in other words, *some* slaveholding is not a sin. How this could be expressed with more rigid accuracy than in my formula of "slavery is not necessarily and in all circumstances sinful," it is for you to show. Why my formula does not more exactly express your belief than your own, which you would substitute for it, is also for you to show. Your statement fails to endure the philosophical test brought forward by yourself. It must have explanations, before the reader can even understand whether it is a universal or particular proposition.

Permit me to add, that even some of your explanations seem to need explanation. For example, in your illustration about the despotism of France, you say that this despotism is "*at the present day,* demanded by the *general good* of the French nation," and then go on to say, that "the time may come when the general good will demand a *different form of government in France.*" Here you propound my doctrine exactly ; and if you will only allow this explanation about despotism to enter into your proposition about slaveholding, it becomes identical with my own. But inasmuch as you insist, that "every general proposition shall be so expressed as to bear examination," "*apart from all explanation,*" you prove that your proposition, as it stands, is not a general, but a particular one, and that mine is really the universal and the philosophical proposition. Again ; your proposition demands explanation, as a practical standard of right conduct as well as of sound philosophy. The proposition, that "slaveholding is not a sin," requires explanation, if you apply the doctrine to the first generation, who, as is generally believed, wrongfully purchased the slaves, and thus abetted manstealing and entailed this unnatural relation upon succeeding generations. It requires explanation, if, anywhere at the South, the good of one or more slaves, and the glory of God, would be promoted by their emancipation. It requires explanation in the Free States, where slavery is prohibited by law, and where the welfare of society does not require the existence of this institution. On the other hand, my proposition that "slavery is not necessarily and in all circumstances sinful" expresses the truth without explanation. No proposition can be expected to define the circumstances

3

under which slavery in every instance may be justified or not. It is sufficient for the purposes of a general statement, to give slave-holding a place among things indifferent (*adiaphora*), and to imply that it is not a permanent institution, based, like marriage, upon the law of God, but one that owes its continuance to the necessities of the public welfare.

3. If the proposition must cover all the ground covered by the doctrine of Christ and his Apostles, then I think that your statement again suffers in comparison with mine. This point has been already discussed. The substance of the scriptural doctrine, in my opinion, is briefly this : First. Slaveholding, in itself considered, is not sinful ; or, it is not a *malum in se*. Secondly. It is a relation of mutual rights and obligations as long as it exists. And, thirdly. The general spirit and precepts of the Gospel are opposed to its perpetuity. I consider that my proposition, in this and in other respects, meets your ethical conditions better than your own.

A third collateral consideration, in favour of my form of stating the scriptural doctrine of Slavery, is, that it commends itself more to the enlightened conscience of the Christian slaveholder.

Christians, whose minds and hearts are imbued with the spirit of their Lord, cannot regard with complacency an institution, whose origin is in wrong, and whose continuance depends upon the inferior condition of a large class of their fellow-men. During my residence at the South, of three years, I do not remember of hearing any justification of slavery, except that which appealed to the actual necessities of the case. It was everywhere said : " The slaves are not fit to be free; neither their own nor the gene-ral welfare would be promoted by immediate emancipation." The lawfulness of continuing the relation under such circumstances could not be called in question. I am confident that the enlight-ened consciences of southern Christians prefer a definition of slavery which includes the providential aspect of the case. No abstract proposition, like yours, will place the vindication of slav-ery on high enough ground to pacify the consciences of those Christians who hold their fellow-men in bondage.

But whilst the language of my statement of the doctrine really justifies, with a high reason, the lawfulness of the relation, if law-ful under the circumstances, the other advantage it has over your statement is in keeping the conscience awake to the obligations of improving the condition of the slaves, with a view to a restoration of their natural rights in a more perfect form of society. If slavery is only to be justified by circumstances, the inquiry must press itself upon the conscience of the Christian master, whether, in the first place, the circumstances and condition of society constitute a sufficient plea, in his judgment, for his present position as a slave-holder ; and in the second place, whether he is doing all he can, as a citizen of the state, and a member of the household of Christ, to remove all unjust enactments from the statute book, and to break down the barriers of intellectual and moral degradation which are in the way of ultimate emancipation. Although "slavery is not necessarily and in all circumstances sinful," it may become so under circumstances where the elevation of the slave concurs with other conditions in rendering his emancipation a benefit.

I claim, therefore, that my statement of the doctrine of slavery surpasses yours, both in its power to relieve the conscience, if charged with the guilt of the existing relation, and in its power to alarm the conscience, if in danger of neglecting the whole duties implied in the relation. My knowledge of southern Christian society gives me boldness in placing this view of the subject before the minds and hearts and consciences of my brethren; for never has it been my privilege to be brought in contact with purer and more devoted servants of our Lord Jesus Christ, than are to be found in the Southern States. With all deference, and in all confidence, I submit to them the truthfulness of the positions taken in this letter.

There is still one more consideration that gives scriptural weight to my form of stating the doctrine of slavery, namely, its *practical power to resist error.*

The fundamental principle of ultra-abolitionism is that slaveholding is in itself sinful. The only efficacious mode of encountering this fanaticism, is to show from the Bible, that it rests upon a false foundation. The doctrines that abolitionism cannot resist, are, first, that the relation itself must neither be confounded with the unjust laws which define the *system*, nor with the inadequate performance of the duties of the relation; and secondly, that slaveholding is not *malum in se*, but right or wrong according to circumstances. This double-edged sword of truth will pierce to the dividing asunder of the bones of rampant abolitionism. Indeed, some of the distinguished leaders of that faction have virtually conceded the scriptural efficiency of these positions, and the great mass of people in the Free States will do homage to their truth. The doctrine that "slavery is not necessarily and in all circumstances sinful," is the contradictory of the abolition dogma; and its establishment in this very form, will most effectually arrest the encroachments of error, and vindicate the cause of righteousness in a perverse generation. Your bare statement, however, that "slaveholding is not a sin in the sight of God," does not meet the case; like a spent arrow, it falls short of the mark. It is a correct statement, to a certain extent; but it does not include providential circumstances, which necessarily enter into the morality of slaveholding. As a weapon to do battle with, your proposition invites assault, without the power to repel. It lacks the scriptural characteristic of fighting a good fight. It carries with it no available and victorious force. It provokes the conscience of the North; it lulls the conscience of the South.

This last sentence indicates an evil on the other extreme. Ultra pro-slavery is as much to be deprecated as ultra anti-slavery. The idea that slaveholding is a divine ordinance, and that it may be lawfully perpetuated to the end of time, is a monstrous doctrine,— derogatory to the spirit and principles of Scripture, to the reason and conscience of mankind, to the universal sway of Providence, and to the glory of Christian civilization. A distinguished slave-holder of the South, who owns several hundred slaves, and who is not a communicant in the Church, after hearing an ultra pro-slavery sermon, came out of the house of God, expressing strong disappro-bation of such sentiments; and, stamping his foot on the ground, declared that he could not endure them. He added that his only justification, before God and the world, for holding slaves, was in the necessities of the case. The attempt to fortify slavery by ex-travagant and unreasonable positions can only do harm. Ex-tremists on one side always beget extremists on the other. Anti-slavery at the North has been the means of developing, to an extent before unknown, ultra pro-slavery at the South. The institu-tion is now claimed, by some, to be a divine ordinance, like mar-riage or civil government; African bondage is sought to be justified by the original diversities of the human race; and even the right eousness of the slave-trade itself is now openly vindicated in this land of liberty and age of light. One strong objection to your state-ment of the doctrine is, that it seems to give countenance to er-roneous and exaggerated views. It will be accepted, I fear, by the ultra pro-slavery party, as a good enough statement to be in-scribed upon their banners. I cordially acquit you of any inten-tion to contribute to the propagation of extreme opinions. But ought not a Presbyterian minister, of your position and influence, to be arrayed against such sentiments, beyond the possibility of misconception? Hitherto, little impression has been made on our Church by ultraists on either side. We at the North are able, with God's blessing, to maintain the scriptural ground against anti-slavery fanaticism; and we ask our brethren at the South to repel the irruptions of pro-slavery fanaticism with equal determination. In order to do this successfully, the South needs a more guarded statement of doctrine than the one you have propounded. That statement is practically inefficacious in resisting ultraism on either side.

For these various reasons, I adhere to the belief that my original proposition on the subject of slaveholding, although not, perhaps, as perfect as it might be, is substantially correct, and is more scriptural and comprehensive than yours.

Yours truly,
C. Van Rensselaer.

REPLY II.

EMANCIPATION AND THE CHURCH.

To the Rev. George D. Armstrong, D.D.:—I certainly did not expect, when I penned the paragraph which you find fault with in your second letter, to become engaged in a controversy about "Emancipation and the Church." My standpoint was that of a private citizen, and I gave utterance to a sentiment, which, I supposed, would find a response in the bosom of any Christian slaveholder on his plantation. The idea of expounding the duty of the Church, in its official capacity, was not in my mind at all. I ask you to look at the plain terms of the paragraph :

"We regard the Christian instruction and elevation of the slaves as a means to an end, and that end is the recovery of the blessings of personal liberty, when Providence shall open the way for it. The higher end is the salvation of their souls."

This paragraph simply declares the Editor's private opinion in regard to the providential antecedents which must necessarily exist, prior to the fitness of the slaves for the blessings of personal liberty. A Christian man ought also, as I supposed, to have the end in view, as well as to keep the means in operation.

I might, perhaps, have fairly declined any formal reply to your second letter, on the ground that you transcended the real intentions of my statement. But inasmuch as the inference you have drawn from it may be a natural one, and is an opinion I really hold, and the arguments, by which you attempt to oppose it, are, in my judgment, unsatisfactory, I shall accept the opportunity of discussing what you seem to insist upon,—the subject of "Emancipation and the Church."

You begin by attempting "to strip the proposition" of what you are pleased to call its "adventitious support." I beg leave, however, to insist that its Christian drapery shall remain upon it, and that it shall retain the firm support of its own Bible truth. The blessings of personal liberty have not been considered by me, in this discussion, in any other sense than including well-being. The whole morality of slaveholding depends upon conditions of social and public welfare, as I have endeavoured to show in my first letter. This is also the fundamental idea in the statement, which you desire to lay violent hands upon. My statement contains three ideas, which ought to be a sufficient guard against the impression that I was in favour of emancipation without an adequate preparation. These three ideas are, *first*, a work of Christian instruction among the slaves; *secondly*, their elevation, as a result of this instruction; and *thirdly*, a progressive condition of society, which, under Providence, would render emancipation practicable and beneficial. Could anything more be expected to render my meaning plain, and to include well-being as an element in the recovery of freedom?

The expression "when Providence shall open the way for it," gives the latitude required in a question of this sort. True well-being was the precise thought in my mind; for, as you justly remark, "Providence never does open the way for any change, unless well-being is to be promoted thereby." Judge, therefore, my surprise, when I find you not only imputing to me the opposite view, but also trying to rob my proposition of the support of divine Providence, whose glorious wisdom and power are so deeply concerned in the solution of this intricate problem. My view of the blessings of personal liberty magnifies well-being. Instead of admitting, therefore, that my statement involves a *petitio principii*, I hold that the real petition is from Dr. Armstrong to alter my proposition to suit his own views. This petition I respectfully decline. I cannot allow any one to banish God and his providence from my meditations on this subject. I choose to retain the whole paragraph, just as it was written, and more particularly the words you desire to exclude.

The terms, "when Providence shall open the way," are used in exactly the same sense as the words "when God in his providence shall open the door for their emancipation,"—an expression employed by the General Assembly of the Presbyterian Church, in 1815, to convey the same idea on the same subject. The question of the time of emancipation is wisely left to the counsels of the Most High. Whether it shall be long, or "before very long," depends, in no inconsiderable degree, so far as human instrumentality is involved, upon the views of those who, like yourself, occupy influential positions in the southern section of the Church. But whether the time be long or short, it will be when "Providence opens the way," or "when God in his providence shall open the door." Not until then, will emancipation be consistent with the true enjoyment of "the blessings of personal liberty." On this particular point, there does not appear to be any real difference of opinion between us.

We also agree in regard to the chief and higher end, which the Christian slaveholder should keep before him. The salvation of the souls of his slaves is the continual burden of a pious master's heart. To be instrumental in bringing to his plantation-household the knowledge of the true God and of redemption by Jesus Christ, is the primary duty and privilege of the relation. No language can exaggerate the magnitude of this responsibility; no enlightened Christian conscience can resist the power of its appeal.

The point on which we differ is, whether the Church has any authority to contemplate emancipation as a righteous and lawful end. This, although a comparatively inferior matter, is nevertheless one of real interest and importance. And, in order that I may not be misunderstood, I request the attention of my brother, Dr. Armstrong, to a few brief explanations.

1. In the first place, an interest, on the part of the Church, in emancipation, does not imply *an undue regard for the temporal, above the spiritual, welfare of the slaves.* The chief duty is to preach " Jesus Christ and Him crucified." No work on earth compares with that of religious teaching and preaching. The vast concerns of immortality should ever be uppermost in the aims and enterprises of the Church. And yet present well-being has such connections with eternal life, as to claim a just share of Christian interest in all generations. The position of the Presbyterian Church has always enabled her to preach the Gospel to both masters and slaves. Ours is not an agitating Church. Her testimony on emancipation, as I shall presently show, has been uttered firmly and fearlessly; but, unlike modern reformers, or other Churches less favoured of heaven, we have not magnified slavery above the higher interests of the kingdom of God, nor substituted vain clamour and restless agitation in the place of "righteousness, peace, and joy in the Holy Ghost."

2. In the second place; to keep in view emancipation as an end, which naturally follows the use of lawful means, *does not bring the Church into the exclusive province of the State.* Slavery has both moral and political aspects. In the letter of the General Assembly to the Presbyterian Church in Ireland, in 1846, the following remarks have a place:

" The relations of negro slavery, as it exists in the States that tolerate it, are twofold. Chiefly, it is an institution purely *civil*, depending absolutely upon the will of the civil power in the States respectively in which it exists : secondarily, it has various aspects and relations, purely or mainly *moral*, in regard to which the several States permit a greater or less degree of intervention."

Our Church has always avoided interference with the State, in matters that are outside of her own appointed work. She has not claimed authority over the political relations of slavery ; nor attempted to extend her domain over subjects not plainly within her own province. It is only where slavery comes within the line of ecclesiastical jurisdiction—that is to say, in its moral and religious aspects, that our Church has maintained her right to deliver her testimony, in such forms, and at such times, as seemed best. She has " rendered unto Cæsar the things that are Cæsar's, and unto God the things that are God's." Let no man attempt to despoil her of this joy.

3. In the third place, the Church's testimony, in favour of emancipation, as a righteous end, must be distinguished from *legislation over the consciences of men.* Testimony differs from ecclesiastical law. It has different objects and purposes, and has a wider latitude of application. A Church judicatory may express its opinions, and attempt to exert its influence in a particular direction, within its lawful sphere, without pretending to make laws to bind the conscience. There are, indeed, duties devolving upon masters, whose violation is justly made the subject of discipline. But there are various views of slavery, which the Church, however desirous of their general adoption among her members, has presented only in the form of opinion, or testimony. Acquiescence in these views, as for example, those on emancipation, has never been made a test of Church communion. Dissenters from testimonies of this nature have no more reason to complain, than the minority in our public bodies have, in general, reason to complain of the decision of the majority on other questions, which come up lawfully for consideration.

4. Emancipation, as an end to be kept in view, *does not imply reproach, where emancipation is, for the present, impracticable.* In my first letter, I have endeavoured to show that slaveholding is not necessarily, and under all circumstances, sinful. There may be conditions of society where the continuance of the relation is among the highest demands of religious obligation. But even in such cases, an enlightened view of duty would, in my judgment, acknowledge emancipation to be an end, worthy of the Gospel of our Lord Jesus Christ. The two ideas of the *lawfulness of the existing relation,* and of the *ultimate end of emancipation,* are perfectly consistent and harmonious. The maintenance of the latter idea conveys no reproach upon the scriptural view of slaveholding. It is antagonistic only to the unscriptural view of the permanence of slavery, as an ordinance of God, on a level with marriage or civil government.

5. The *time* of emancipation, as I have already intimated, the Church has left to the decisions of Providence. Circumstances vary so much in society, that no rule can have a universal application. It is sufficient to keep emancipation in view, and to labour to secure its attainment as speedily as circumstances will permit, or " when Providence shall open the way."

Having made these explanations in the hope of disarming prejudice and conciliating good-will, I shall proceed to show, first, that my views of "Emancipation and the Church" are sustained by the testimony of the General Assembly, whilst yours differ from it; and secondly, that the testimony of our Church is sustained by the Word of God.

The TESTIMONY OF THE GENERAL ASSEMBLY on emancipation is

important, as an exhibition of the general sentiments of the Presbyterian Church on this great social question, and particularly as showing its interpretation of the Scriptures.

The first deliverance of our Church on the subject, was made in the year 1787, by the Synod of New York and Philadelphia, which was at that time our highest judicatory, and was in the act of forming our present ecclesiastical constitution.

The deliverance is as follows:

"The Synod of New York and Philadelphia do highly approve of the general principles in favour of universal liberty that prevail in America, and the interest which many of the States have taken in promoting the abolition of slavery; yet, inasmuch as men, introduced from a servile state, to a participation of all the privileges of civil society without a proper education, and without previous habits of industry, may be in many respects dangerous to the community; therefore, they earnestly recommend it to all the members belonging to their communion, to give those persons who are at present held in servitude, such good education as to *prepare them for the better enjoyment of freedom;* and they moreover recommend that masters, whenever they find servants disposed to make a just improvement of the privilege, would give them *a peculium,* or grant them sufficient time and sufficient means of procuring their own liberty, at a moderate rate; that thereby they may be brought into society with those habits of industry that may render them useful citizens; and finally, they recommend it to all their people to use the most prudent measures consistent with the interests and the state of civil society, in the countries where they live, to *procure eventually the final abolition of slavery in America.*"

In 1793, this judgment was reaffirmed by the General Assembly, and again reiterated by the Assembly in 1795, with the remark that "*they trust every conscientious person will be fully satisfied with it.*" Its brevity, its comprehensiveness, its conservative tone, and its scriptural authority, make this testimony deserving of great attention. The General Assembly, in 1815, testified to the same effect:

"The General Assembly have repeatedly declared their cordial approbation of those principles of civil liberty, which appear to be recognized by the Federal and State Governments in these United States. They have expressed their regret that the slavery of the Africans, and of their descendants, still continues in so many places, and even among those within the pale of the Church, and have urged the Presbyteries under their care to adopt such measures as will secure, at least, to the rising generation of slaves within the bounds of the Church, a religious education, that *they may be prepared for the exercise and enjoyment of liberty, when God, in his providence, may open the door for their emancipation.*"

It could hardly be expected that a deliverance could be found on the records of our Church, so exactly concurring in thought and language with the extemporaneous statement contained in my brief review.

In 1818, the largest Assembly that had yet been convened, met in Philadelphia. An abler body of divines, probably, never assembled in our highest judicatory. The paper adopted by them, on the subject of slavery, is too well known to require large extracts. It was drawn up by Dr. Ashbel Green, with the concurrence of Dr. George A. Baxter, of your own Synod. Dr. Speece, of Virginia, was Dr. Baxter's fellow-commissioner from your old Presbytery of Lexington. I only quote a few sentences from this celebrated document.

"We rejoice that the Church to which we belong, commenced as early as any other in this country, the good work of *endeavouring to put an end to slavery,* and that in the same work, many of its members have ever since been, and now are among the most active, efficient, and vigorous labourers."

"At the same time, we earnestly exhort them to *continue, and, if possible, to increase* their exertions to effect a total abolition of slavery. We exhort them to suffer no greater delay to take place in this most interesting concern, than a regard to the public welfare truly and indispensably demands."

"We, therefore, warn all who belong to our denomination of Christians, against unduly extending this plea of necessity; against making it a cover for the love and practice of slavery, or a pretence for *not using efforts that are lawful and practicable,* to extinguish this evil.

"And we at the same time exhort others to forbear harsh censures, and uncharitable reflections on their brethren, who unhappily live among slaves, whom they cannot immediately set free, but who are *really using all of their influence and all their endeavours* to bring them into a state of freedom, *as soon as a door for it can be safely opened."**

The General Assembly, in 1845, took action on the specific point, whether slaveholding was, under all circumstances, a bar to Christian communion; and in 1846 reaffirmed all the testimony uttered by preceding General Assemblies.

Here I might rest the case, so far as your opposition to the recorded views of our Church needed any demonstration; but as you are *now* a Virginian, I cannot avoid inviting your attention to the testimony of the Synod of Virginia in 1800. Half a century has, indeed, passed by, and many of the precious men of God, who then served the churches from Lexington to Norfolk, have ceased from their labours; but the record of their opinions will endure throughout all generations.

This subject was brought before the Synod of Virginia by a memorial on emancipation, from one of their congregations. The

---

* The Assembly's testimony of 1818 was reaffirmed at the *last meeting of the Synods of Pittsburg and Ohio.* These two Synods, in the midst of which the Western Theological Seminary stands, have been denominated " the back bone of Presbyterianism." The testimony of 1818 contains some expressions which might be advantageously altered; but, with the proper explanations, it is consistent with that of 1845. The parts I have quoted have not been excepted to, so far as I know.

following extracts are from the answer returned by the Synod to the memorial.

"That so many thousands of our fellow-creatures should, in this land of liberty and asylum for the oppressed, be held in chains, is a reflection to us painfully afflictive. And most earnestly do we wish that all the members of our communion would pay a proper attention to the recommendation of the late Synod of New York and Philadelphia upon this subject. We consider it the indispensable duty of all who hold slaves to *prepare, by a suitable education, the young among them for a state of freedom, and to liberate them as soon as they shall appear to be duly qualified for that high privilege;* and such as neglect a duty so evidently and so powerfully enforced by the common principles of justice, as well as by the dictates of humanity, and the benign genius of our holy religion, ought, in our opinion, to be seriously dealt with and admonished on that account. But to refuse to hold Christian communion with any who may differ from us in sentiment and practice in this instance, would, we conceive, in the present conjuncture at least, be a very unwarrantable procedure; a direct infraction of the decision of the General Assembly of our Church, and a manifest departure from the practice of the Apostles and the primitive Church."

"That it was wrong in the first instance to reduce so many of the helpless Africans to their present state of thraldom will be readily admitted, and that it is a duty to adopt proper measures for *their emancipation, will, it is presumed, be universally conceded.* But, with respect to the measures best calculated to accomplish that important purpose, and the time necessary to give them full effect, different sentiments may be entertained by the true disciples of the Great Friend of man."*

The Synod of Virginia probably entertain the same sentiments in 1858; and, if the occasion required it, would doubtless reaffirm this testimony, with the same love to Christ that originated it in the days of Waddell, Legrand, Rice, Alexander, Lacy, Hoge, Lyle, Brown, Baxter, Houston, &c.,—a generation of revered men, "mighty in the Scriptures."

It is clear that my statement concerning "Emancipation and the Church" is no novelty, but that it is regular, orthodox, old-fashioned, Presbyterian truth.

SECONDLY. I further maintain, that this truth is scriptural truth; and, that the Church has a right to propose, and to hold forth, emancipation as a righteous end, when Providence shall open the way.

Here, I am met, at once, by your declaration, that

"The word of God contains no deliverance, express or clearly implied, respecting emancipation. Hence, I affirm, that the

---

* Quoted from "THE HAND BOOK OF SLAVERY," by the Rev. John Robinson, of Ashland, Ohio. Published by John D. Thorpe, Cincinnati, 1852. This is one of the best books on the subject yet published, containing much valuable information and able discussion.

Church has no right to make a deliverance respecting it; much less to set it before herself as an end of her labours."

In examining this proposition, I venture to lay down the following, as a counter proposition in part, and as a more scriptural view of the subject; viz.: The Church has a right to expound, and to apply, the word of God, in reference to all the relations of life, and to all the changing aspects of society. The exposition and application must, of course, be consistent with the spirit and principles of the Bible, but they are not limited to the mere word of its letter, nor to any general or universal formula of expression. From the nature of the case, exposition requires enlargement of scriptural statement, and application implies a regard to providential developments and to the varying circumstances of social and public life. Paul's Epistle to the Corinthians was very different from his Epistles to the Romans and to the Hebrews, although they all contained expositions of the same scriptural doctrines; and his Epistle to Philemon contained a new application, in the case of Onesimus, of principles, not previously so fully developed. The Church has, in every age, the right to expound the sacred Scriptures according to the light granted by the Holy Spirit, and to apply its interpretation to all cases, judged to be within its spiritual jurisdiction.

I. Let us, in this search after Bible truth, glance at some of the views of the *Old Testament Scriptures*, on slavery and emancipation.

A terrific statute flashed out from Sinai into the legislation of the Hebrew commonwealth. By the laws of Moses, "He that stealeth a man, and selleth him, or if he be found in his hands, he shall surely be put to death." (Ex. 21 : 16.) The original man-stealer, and the receiver of the stolen person, were both to suffer the penalty of death. The operation of this single statute would have forever excluded the existence of American slavery.

Another provision, of some significance, shone with benignant beams of liberty. A fugitive slave, from a foreign country, was not to be sent back into slavery. (Deut. 23 : 15, 16.) The Hebrew commonwealth was a city of refuge and an asylum of liberty to the surrounding nations. These two statutes stood, like Jachin and Boaz, at the vestibule of the Mosaic legislation on slavery.

Hebrew bondmen were held under a system, which resembled, in its nature, hired service rather than slavery, and whose duration was limited. Hebrew servants were emancipated on the seventh year, except in cases of voluntary agreement, and of children born under certain circumstances. In the year of Jubilee, liberty was proclaimed " unto all the inhabitants of the land." (Lev. 25 : 10.) In the fiftieth year, every Hebrew " returned unto his family," under the protection of a great festival statute.*

---

* There are differences of opinion about the extent of emancipation, on the year of

The Old Testament dispensation made distinctions between the Israelites and Gentiles, in various parts of its legislation, and, among others, on slavery. Bondmen, purchased by the Hebrews from the Gentiles, might be held in perpetuity. Their bondage, however, as Dr. Spring remarks, partook of the character of apprenticeship, rather than of rigorous servitude.

The great fact remains prominent, that the bondage of *Hebrews* was temporary. Emancipation was continually in sight; and the effect of their septennial and jubilee emancipation periods must have been a moral check and rebuke to slavery, under whatever forms it was tolerated.

The long-existing middle wall of partition between Jews and Gentiles, was at length overthrown by Christianity. Thenceforward, all mankind stood in the new relation of a common brotherhood. "There is neither Jew nor Greek, there is neither bond nor free, there is neither male nor female; for ye are all one in Christ Jesus. And if ye be Christ's, then are ye Abraham's seed, and heirs according to the promise." (Gal. 3:28, 29.) Timothy, who, from a child, had known the Holy Scriptures, must have realized, with all pious Jews, that the spirit of the Old Testament no longer sanctioned the holding of even *Gentile* brethren, in *perpetual* bondage. All laws, peculiar to the Jewish economy, being now abolished, the New Testament, in its larger spirit and greater light, was brought into contact with the arbitrary slavery of the Pagan nations. Can it be believed that, under these circumstances, any well-instructed Jewish Christians would become voluntarily involved in the pagan system of slavery? Heathen slaveholders, on their becoming Christians, received instructions, which gave new views of their obligations, and which tended to the ultimate abolition of the system.

II. Christianity, in reforming the evils of society, inculcated general principles, of far greater influence than positive Mosaic laws. Before examining the true tendency of some of these scriptural principles, I shall ask your attention to the doctrine, which Paul expounded to the Corinthian slaves. "Art thou called, being a servant, or slave, care not for it. *But if thou mayst be made free,* USE IT RATHER." (1 Cor. 7:21.)

The ideas that are fairly implied in this verse are the following:
1. Religion is the most precious of all blessings to mankind.

Jubilee. Some suppose that *all* the slaves, whether Hebrews or Gentiles, were then set free; others suppose that not even all the *Hebrews* were emancipated. My own opinion is, that the Jubilee was for the *Hebrews* alone, and that it emancipated *all* the Hebrew bondmen. The only doubt is in reference to those Hebrews, who became voluntary bondmen, and whose ears were bored in token of their submission. But Josephus, Maimonides, Calvin, Michælis, &c., include these among those set free at the fiftieth year, and maintain that the Jubilee period gave to the Hebrews universal emancipation. Even if an exception is to be made, of the comparatively few cases of *voluntary,* ear-bored, bondmen for life, the argument is not materially affected.

The Lord's freeman may bear, with little anxiety, any external condition of life, even though it be that of bondage. Well may Presbyterians rejoice that their Church, in conformity to apostolic precept and practice, has preached the Gospel to the slaves, without unduly agitating points bearing on their temporal welfare.

2. Slavery is an abnormal, and not a permanent, condition. Paul exhorted Christian slaves to seek emancipation, if within their reach, or if Providence opened the way for it. It is impossible to reconcile this inspired passage with the theory that slavery, like civil government or marriage, is an ordinance of God, to be perpetuated forever. "Use your freedom, rather," says Paul, expounding the nature of slavery, and throwing the light of inspiration upon its anomalous character. When did the Apostle ever exhort husbands and wives not to care for the marriage tie, and to seek to be free from it, if the opportunity offered ? Slavery was in its nature a temporary expedient, differing from marriage, which is founded upon the natural and permanent relations of life. Slavery is limited in its duration by the very conditions of its lawful existence.

3. The Apostle teaches the Corinthian slaves that liberty is a higher and better condition than bondage. Although Christian slaves ought to be submissive to their lot, they have a right to regard liberty as a greater blessing. CALVIN, our great commentator, says: "Paul means to intimate that liberty is not merely good, but also *more advantageous than servitude.* If he is speaking to servants, his meaning will be this : While I exhort you to be free from anxiety, I do not hinder you from even availing yourselves of liberty, if a [lawful] opportunity presents itself to you. If he is addressing himself to those who are free, it will be a kind of concession, as though he had said,—I exhort servants to be of good courage, though a state of freedom is preferable,* and more to be desired, if one has it in his choice." The Apostle evidently considered liberty to be the highest state, offering an advance in civilization and true well-being, when Providence opens the way.

4. Paul also maintains that emancipation is an object of Christian desire, when it can be lawfully secured. Our own great commentator, Dr. HODGE, says : "Paul's object is not to exhort men not to improve their condition, but simply not to allow their social relations to disturb them ; or imagine that their becoming Christians rendered it necessary to change those relations. He could, with perfect consistency with the context, say to the slave, 'Let not your being a slave give you any concern ; but if you can become free, choose freedom rather than slavery.' Luther, Calvin, Beza, and the great body of commentators, from their day to this, understood the Apostle to say that liberty was to be chosen, if the opportunity to become free were offered."

---

* "Soit *beaucoup* meilleur"—" is *much* better."

Now, if the great Apostle to the Gentiles taught that slavery is an inferior condition, and that, under right circumstances, emancipation is a lawful object of Christian desire, may not the Church teach the same things? Whilst the highest and chief end is to lead the slaves to Christ and to heaven, is the Church compelled to abjure all other ends, relating to human happiness, elevation, and liberty? Far from it. Paul's doctrine to Timothy, upon which you lay so much stress, must not be expounded to the exclusion of Paul's doctrine to the Corinthians.

Christian masters are informed, in this passage, that their slaves may rightly regard their bondage as an inferior state, which may be superseded in due time; and the masters themselves are thus, incidentally, instructed to keep emancipation in view, and to prepare the slaves for it, when the providential opportunity arrives.

Further. If emancipation be a good which slaves may lawfully desire, it is a good which *all Christians* may lawfully desire, and labour, according to their opportunity, to *confer upon them*. It is not, indeed, in such a sense an absolute good that it may not be abused, or that every class of people is always prepared safely to possess it. The same is true of the self-control which the law confers upon children, on reaching their majority. But is this any reason why children should not desire to be their own masters at a suitable age, or why all should not desire and labour so to train them that they may be duly prepared, at the fit time, to be invested with self-control?

You refer me to the explanations of your book on this passage in the Epistle to the Corinthians. The explanations I find to be twofold: First, you urge that slavery in Greece and Rome was far more rigorous than in our Southern States; and secondly, that the Africans and Anglo-Saxons belong to different races; and that, on these two accounts, the doctrine of Paul has a less forcible application to American than to Corinthian slaves. I cheerfully yield to your argument any benefit which may be fairly claimed by a change of circumstances; but I submit, in reply, *first*, that human nature is the same in all ages and nations, and has natural desires to embrace every lawful opportunity to improve its outward condition; *secondly*, that the Apostle propounds a principle, which has a real bearing upon slavery at all times and everywhere; *thirdly*, that the light, liberty, and Christian appliances of the nineteenth century, are an offset against the supposed advantages for emancipation possessed by ancient Greece and Rome; and *fourthly*, that your apology for not fully applying the principle to slavery now, as well as to slavery eighteen hundred years ago, is at least a virtual acquiescence, however feeble, in the truth of Paul's doctrine.—I find, indeed, on recurring to your book, that Dr. Armstrong expounds the passage admirably. You say: "Yet, if they can lawfully be made free, *as a general rule*, slaves had better accept their freedom; for a condition of slavery is not to be desired on its own account." p. 67. This is substantially the " Christian doctrine" I am advocating ; but how a Christian minister can reconcile this scriptural view of the subject with the silent and unchallenged expression of all sorts of opinions about the perpetuity, desirableness, &c., of slavery, I leave others to determine. Slavery was no less a political institution in the days of Paul than it is now. Is the Church, therefore, to be perpetually silent, as though slavery possessed no moral relations to the law of God? Is it exclusively a question of " capital and labour ?" Surely, the Church may follow Paul in his inspired expositions, although his Epistles contain some things "hard to be understood," and easy to " wrest."

III. Paul's incidental interpretation of the law of liberty to the Corinthian slaves, is in entire accordance with the *injunctions of Scripture*. Slaveholding is not in itself sinful, but its existence binds upon masters and slaves mutual obligations, whose tendency is to abolish eventually the entire system. If the Scriptures enjoin what, of necessity, leads to emancipation, they enjoin emancipation itself, when the time comes ; if they forbid what is necessary to the perpetuity of slavery, they forbid that slavery should be perpetuated.

How, then, do these divine injunctions to masters and slaves operate against the perpetuity of slavery?

1. Christianity requires the *kind personal treatment* of the slaves ; it removes the rigours of bondage, and insensibly assimilates the system to one of apprenticeship. Religious obligation is made the basis of all the duties of the relation. There is a " Master in Heaven," who rules over all ; who searches the hearts of all ; who weighs the actions of all ; and who keeps a record for the final judgment. "The Bible method," says Dr. Hodge, " of dealing with slavery and similar institutions, is to enforce, on all concerned, the *great principles of moral obligation*—assured that those principles, if allowed free scope, will put an end to all the evils both in the political and social relations of men." " First, the evils of slavery, and then slavery itself, would pass away as naturally and as healthfully as children cease to be minors." The kind treatment which the Gospel requires towards slaves, and the corresponding obligations of slaves to their masters, cultivate feelings of mutual regard, which open the way for everything good in due time.

2. The effect of Christianity upon the sanctity of *the marriage state* is of the same preparatory nature. The law of Eden regulates social life everywhere ; it protects husbands and wives on the plantation in their relations to each other and their children. The husband is " the head of the wife, as Christ is the head of the Church." " As the Church is subject to Christ, so let the wives be to their own husbands in everything." Forcible disruptions of the mar-

riage bond by sale, or by separation for life, are not authorized by the word of God. The Christian law of marriage holds inviolate the sacred privacies of home; and the very difficulties of fulfilling the obligations of this law in a state of bondage, are suggestions in behalf of the natural state of liberty.

3. The Gospel demands an *adequate compensation of service.* "The labourer is worthy of his hire," whether he be a minister of the sanctuary or a plantation slave. He is entitled to food, raiment, and shelter, and to whatever additional remuneration and privilege justice demands, in view of all the circumstances in each case. This doctrine of equitable compensation gradually unsettles the arbitrary or despotic nature of the relation, and provides a natural progress towards the coming end.

4. Religion protects the *avails of human industry;* it favours the right of every man to the fruits of his labour. The laws of the State deny, in general, the right of slaves to any property; but the Bible enjoins that which is "just and equal." In practice, Christian masters generally acknowledge, in a greater or less degree, the justice of this claim. Such a practice is a scriptural auxiliary to final emancipation. Ideas of property enlarge the mind, cherish thoughts of independence, cultivate habits of industry, and possess a stimulating power upon the general character of the slave, which fits him for the exercise of all the rights of liberty, "when Providence shall open the way."

5. The *intellectual and moral elevation* of the slaves is a necessary result of Christian treatment and instruction. The Bible is the universal text-book for mankind. Religious knowledge introduces all other knowledge. Any system that depends for its support upon the ignorance and debasement of the people, is doomed, by the law of Providence, to extinction. It was the wish of a pious king that every man in his dominions might be able to read the Bible. A Christian slaveholder, in like manner realizes the obligations to give instruction to the slaves in his household. Religion tends to knowledge and virtue; and knowledge and virtue tend to liberty.

If these statements are correct, obedience to the special injunctions of the Bible, on the subject of slavery, tends to, and necessarily terminates in, Emancipation. The Church, therefore, may scripturally keep in view this great moral result, to the glory of her heavenly King.

IV. I add, that the *universal spirit and fundamental principles of religion* originate, and foster, sentiments favourable to the natural rights of mankind. Born of the same race, inheritors of the same corrupt nature, heirs of the same Divine promises, partakers of the same redemption in Jesus Christ, subjects of the same resurrection from the dead, and if saved, inhabitants of the same

mansions of glory and immortality, the children of bondage are elevated by the Bible to a condition of co-equal spiritual dignity, that
asserts, and must ultimately obtain, the full recognition of all their
rights.

Love to God and love to man, is the substance of the Divine requirements. " Thou shalt love thy neighbour as thyself ;" " All
things whatsoever ye would that men should do to you, do ye even
so unto them." I am aware of the fanatical and unscriptural in-
terpretations that have been sometimes put upon the great law of
Christian reciprocity. I disclaim fellowship with unreasonable and
false dogmas. But I think that the fair, scriptural interpretation
of the rule of love bears irresistibly against the *perpetuity of slavery*,
as well as against its rash or precipitate overthrow. Christianity
seeks to adjust the condition of society, on a basis of universal
brotherhood, fitted to accomplish the sublime purposes of " peace
on earth, and good-will towards men."

In all periods of her history, the Church has identified herself
with the well-being of the masses. Without interfering with political relations, she has never renounced her interest in the highest
welfare of the human race, both in this life and the life to come.
At the present day, the Presbyterian Church, in preaching the
Gospel to the heathen, expends a part of her resources in sending
physicians to heal their diseases, farmers to assist in agricultural
management, mechanics to work at printing-presses, teachers to
instruct in schools. The principle actuating this general policy
is, that the temporal well-being of mankind is, within certain limits,
directly auxiliary to the preaching of the Gospel and the salvation
of souls. So far as slavery is a question of " capital and labour,"
or so far as emancipation depends upon the laws of the State,
ecclesiastical authority is impertinent ; but the moral results to be
secured by the elevation and emancipation of the slaves, are within
the true aim of the law of love and of Gospel grace.

Can it be "extra-scriptural, unscriptural, and anti-scriptural,"
for the Church, besides seeking the eternal salvation of the slaves,
to endeavour to introduce them to the blessings of personal liberty,
" when Providence shall open the way ?" Certainly, nothing less
than this result is to be desired, when Providence shall so arrange
and prepare things, that the welfare of society and the claims of
justice and mercy shall require the termination of involuntary servitude. This supposes a great advance in the intellectual, moral,
and religious condition of the slaves. Is it sinful to desire, and
pray, and labour for such a state of things ? If so, I confess myself
ignorant of the first principles of the doctrine of Christ.

In bringing this long Letter to a close, I must ask your attention
to one or two more things.

If the Scriptures do not contain any deliverance on this subject, either "express or clearly implied," then the Christian, as a *citizen*, has no divine rule to guide his conduct. Emancipation, if it comes at all, comes not as a desired end, but as a mere incident. The whole question, with its moralities and economics, is left to the operation of natural laws. If not a scriptural end, it may, or may not, be reckoned within the range of private and public prayer, and of earnest Christian enterprise and activity. If "extra-scriptural, unscriptural, and anti-scriptural," might not some infer that it was *sinful?* The motives that lead men to glorify God in labouring to remove social evils, are thus impaired in their force, if not rendered inoperative in this particular sphere. The effect of such doctrine in perpetuating slavery, cannot be concealed or denied.

If I understand you, emancipation in *Liberia* is acknowledged to be a proper object of ecclesiastical action, for the reason, among others, that it passes by the question of "the general ultimate emancipation of the slaves" in *this country.* But is not the principle the same, wherever the result may be finally secured? My statement leaves the time, place, and circumstances of emancipation to the Providence of God; whilst your view seems to admit the lawfulness of the end, provided that you yourself locate and define the land of liberty. Is not this a virtual surrender of the principle contained in your argument? In your general sentiments on Liberian Colonization, I cordially concur.

One of the most painful things, allow me to say fraternally, in your Letter, is the low view of the natural rights of mankind, which pervades the discussion. I fully acknowledge the difficulties of emancipation, and most truly sympathize with my brethren, in Church and State, who are involved in the evils of this complicated system. But if we lose sight of, or depreciate principles, difficulties and dangers will increase on every side. Are there no eternal principles of justice, no standard of human rights, by which a system of servitude shall submit to be judged, and in whose presence it shall be made to plead for justification? Is civil liberty a mere abstraction? Thanks be to God, the Presbyterian Church has been the advocate of freedom in every land and age. Long may she maintain this position of truth and righteousness, in the spirit of good-will to all men, bond and free; and whilst she holds that slavery is not necessarily and in all circumstances sinful, may her testimony against the evils of the system, and in favour of emancipation, be clear, consistent, and unwavering, before God and the world!

Presbyterians at the North have remained steadfast in their integrity, amidst all the abolition agitation which has threatened injury, and even destruction, to the Church. We have deprecated this agitation, not simply on account of its own perverse nature, but on account of its evil influence in provoking extreme views among our brethren at the South. The northern section of the Church, by its successful resistance to fanaticism, earnestly and fraternally appeals to the Presbyterians at the South, to remain equally true to the principles and the testimonies sanctioned by the unanimous voice of our General Assemblies, and by the higher authority of the Sacred Scriptures.

I am yours, truly,

C. VAN RENSSELAER.

REPLY III.

To the Rev. George D. Armstrong, D.D.:—History teaches important lessons; but I have several objections to the historical view presented in your letter as the basis of instruction.

1. One of the forms of historical statement, liable to misconception, is that the Apostles maintained without qualification, that " *slaveholding is not a sin.*" This mode of stating the doctrine is not, in my opinion, precisely scriptural. It leaves the impression that slavery is, always and everywhere, a lawful institution. All that the Scriptures authorize us to affirm, as I have endeavoured to show in my first letter, is that slaveholding is not a *malum in se*, or in other words, that it is right or wrong, according to circumstances. As this point lies at the basis of your historical sketch, I have deemed it important to notice it at the very beginning.

2. In the second place, the assertion that " *slavery continued to exist everywhere,*" is no evidence that Christianity everywhere approved of it. Despotism and war prevailed in early times; and although they still continue to exist throughout the world, the spirit of true religion has always been in opposition to their perpetuity. The simple fact of the long continuance of such an institution as slavery cannot be interpreted into a divine warrant.

3. In the third place, your historical statement entirely overlooks the *early influence of Christianity upon slavery*.

The religion of Christ was, for a long period, subjected to fierce persecutions, and rejected from the councils of the Roman Empire. When it finally secured a temporary triumph under Constantine, corruption almost simultaneously began its work. There are, nevertheless, many evidences of an advancing social and political movement, in the mitigation of the evils of slavery and in the measures of emancipation. From the first, " the humane spirit of our religion struggled with the customs and manners of this world, and contributed more than any other circumstance, to introduce the practice of manumission."* Christianity ameliorated the condition of slaves under the Roman Government, inclined Constantine to render their emancipation much easier than formerly, and awakened a religious interest in the subject. " As slaves were formerly declared to be emancipated in the temple of the

* Robertson.

goddess Feronia, so afterwards, in accordance with the decrees of Constantine, they were throughout the Roman Empire, *set free in the churches.*"* Sozomen, speaking of Constantine, says: " In reference to the bestowment of the better liberty (viz., Roman citizenship), he laid down these laws, decreeing that *all, emancipated in the Church under the direction of the priests*, should enjoy Roman citizenship."† The Church sometimes paid for the ransom of slaves, especially for slaves or captives subjected to heathen or barbarian masters. " Out of the legitimate work of the faithful," say the Apostolic Constitutions, "deliver the saints, redeem the slaves, the captives,"‡ &c. Ignatius alludes likewise to the redeemed slaves at the expense of the community.§ Clement of Rome also speaks of Christians who carried devotion so far as to sell themselves to redeem others from slavery.‖

Large numbers of slaves were emancipated in the first ages of Christianity. One of our own distinguished writers, whose position, intellectual habits, and course of investigation have enabled him to give much attention to this subject, has the following remarks :

" Before the advent of Christianity, no axe had ever been laid at the root of slavery ; no philosopher had denounced it, and it does not appear to have been considered by any as an evil to be repressed. Nor did the apostles teach differently, but distinctly laid down rules for the conduct of master and slave ; thereby clearly recognizing the relation, without denouncing it as in itself sinful. Their Master's instructions were intended to make men what they should be, and then every institution, every law, and every practice inconsistent with that state, would fall before it. If a community of slaveholders, under Christian instruction, were gradually tending to the point of general emancipation, both masters and slaves would gradually be fitting for so great a change in their relative condition. It would be a subject of great interest to trace, in the early ages of Christianity, its influences upon the institution of slavery, so much in contrast with the movements or influences of paganism. During the first four or five centuries of the Christian era, *emancipation of slaves by converts to Christianity took place upon a large and progressively increasing scale*, and continued until the occurrence of political events, the invasion of barbarians, and other causes, agitated the whole Christian world, and shook the very foundations of the social systems in which Christianity had made most progress. When Christianity sank into the darkness of the middle ages, the progress of emancipation ceased, because the influence which produced it ceased during that period to operate. The annals of emancipation in these primitive ages, if materials were extant for a full narrative, would be of extraordinary interest, and would fully reveal the effects of our Saviour's precepts when brought to bear upon the hearts of men in their true spirit, even where the letter did not apply. Under paganism, slavery could never come to an end : under the continual light of Christianity, it hastens to an inevitable end, but by that

---

* Can. 64, Cod. Eccl. Africanæ.   † Sozomenus, lib. 1; Hist. Eccl. Chap. IX.
‡ IV. 9.   § Ep. ad Polyc. c. 4.   ‖ 1 Ep. ad Cor.

progress and in that mode which is best both for master and slave ; both being bound to love each other, until the door of emancipation is fully open without injury to either."*

In addition to these interesting statements from Mr. Colwell, I offer to your consideration the following extracts from the admirable work of the Rev. STEPHEN CHASTEL, of Geneva, on the " Charity of the Primitive Churches."†

" Between the Christian master and slave was no religious distinction ; they came into the same sanctuary to invoke the same God, to pray, to sing together, to participate in the same mysteries, to sit at the same table, to drink of the same cup, and to take part in the same feast. How should this community of worship not have profoundly modified their mutual relations ? How could the master have continued to see in his slave that *thing* which the Roman law permitted him to *use* and to *abuse ?* Also, whatever might still be the force of habit and of manners, there were rarely seen in the Christian houses those masters, still less those pitiless mistresses, such as Seneca and Juvenal have painted to us ; the slave, there, had to fear neither the cross, nor tortures, nor abandonment in sickness, nor to be thrown off in his old age ; he had not to fear that he should be sold for the amphitheatre, or for some one of those infamous occupations which the Church reproved, and from which she struggled, at every price, to rescue her children.

" Finally, a devoted and faithful slave always had, in a Christian house, the hope of recovering his liberty. It was not rare, without doubt, to see Pagans enfranchise their slaves ; some even did it from motives of gratitude or attachment ; but ordinarily necessity, caprice, vanity, often even the most sordid calculations alone presided over the emancipation of slaves, and these miserable creatures, cast almost without resource into the midst of a society whose free labour found so little encouragement and employment, hardly used their liberty except to do evil, and went for the most part to increase the crowd of proletarians and of beggars, so that it is not astonishing if the emperors had attempted, though without success, to limit, by their laws, the right of enfranchising. As to the Church, when she encouraged it, it was not as an interest, but as a favour ; she exhorted the masters to liberate the slave as often as he was in a state to support himself. But the enfranchisement was not an abandonment ; the Christian remained the *patron*, in the best sense of that word, of those whom he had ceased to be the master of, and, in case of misfortune, the freed man found an almost sure resource in the aid of his brothers. The Church, which, by its moral influence, had worked to render him worthy of liberty, continued to protect him after he had attained it. The emancipation of slaves at this day would be less difficult and less dangerous if it was always done in this spirit."‡

* New Themes for the Protestant Clergy, by STEPHEN COLWELL, Esq.

† Translated by Professor Matile, and published by J. B. Lippincott & Co., Philadelphia, 1857.

‡ The Church has been thus unjustly accused of having, by the imprudence of her emancipations of slaves, caused the plague of pauperism. Manumission had been used with much less discretion at other epochs of Roman society. The one hundred thousand freedmen who, as early as from 240 to 210 previous to our era had been

The " correctness" of these brief accounts of the early impression of Christianity upon slavery, "no one, I presume, will call in question ;" and they stand in delightful contrast with the injurious and unhistorical representations, quoted in your Letter from Dr. Hopkins, Bishop of the Episcopal Church of Vermont.

4. I take exception to the statement that slaves were always " *held, without any reproach, even by the bishops and clergy,*" down to the period of the abolition of slavery in Europe. Undoubtedly, slaves might have been held, without any reproach, then as now, when the circumstances of society and the welfare of the slaves justified the continuance of the relation. The fact that, under Constantine, emancipation took place in the churches, shows that the act was regarded as peculiarly congenial with the spirit and principles of religion. Ward, in his Law of Nations, observes that "it is of little consequence to object that the custom of slavery remained for a great length of time, or that the Church itself was possessed of numbers of slaves. The custom of enfranchisement was the effect, chiefly, of pious and Christian motives, and the *example was generally set by the ministers of religion.*"

The same writer observes, in reference to later times, that, " in the opinion of Grotius, Christianity was the great and almost only cause of abolition. The professed and assigned reasons for most of the charters of manumissions, from the time of Gregory the Great [A.D. 600] to the thirteenth century, were the religious and pious considerations of the fraternity of men, the imitation of the example of Christ, the love of our Maker, and the hope of redemption. Enfranchisement was frequently given on a deathbed, as the most acceptable service that could be offered ; and when the sacred character of the priesthood came to obtain more universal veneration, *to assume its functions was the immediate passport to freedom.*"

History does not at all warrant the assertion that slaves have been always held " without any reproach." From the earliest period, the anomalous character of the relation, and its attending evils, have been recorded on the impartial, but obscure annals of the past. Not even in the dark middle ages was slavery ranked among irreproachable and permanent institutions.

5. Another error in your historical sketch is, that, when the practice of slavery "died out" in Europe, the change was "*through the operation of worldly causes.*" It is surprising that two bishops of the Church should agree upon a statement, disowning the con-

admitted to the privilege of citizenship, the slaves liberated *en masse* by the alternating politics of Marius and Sylla, the thousands of them who under the republic were daily liberated, either by will, to do honour to the funeral of their master, or by necessity, there being no food for them, or by revenge, to defeat the eagerness of creditors; all those freedmen, finally, who in Cicero's times were in a majority in the urban and rural tribes of Rome, formed elements much more threatening to the social well-being than were subsequently those freed by charity. (Moreau-Christophe, *Du probl. de la misère*, Vol. I, p. 80, etc.)

nection between Christianity and the removal of this great social evil. The changes introduced into society, in the progress of advancing civilization, have been hitherto ascribed by all Christian writers to the power of Christianity itself. But in the nineteenth century, the theory is advanced, that "worldly causes," and not religion, have been the efficient agents in the extinction of slavery! If this be true in all previous ages, the inference is that it will be so in all time to come. This is a "short and easy method" of establishing ultra pro-slavery doctrine. But is the statement true? In addition to the testimony already adduced, which has a bearing upon this point, I venture to ask your attention to the following remarks, contained in the volumes of Mr. Bancroft, the historian. You will observe the prominence given to *religion*, by this distinguished writer.

"In defiance of severe penalties, the Saxons sold their own kindred into slavery on the continent; nor could the traffic be checked, till *religion*, pleading the cause of humanity, made its appeal to *conscience*."*

"What though the trade was exposed to the *censure of the Church*, and prohibited by the laws of Venice? It could not be effectually checked, till, by the Venitian law, no slave might enter a Venitian ship, and to tread the deck of an argosy of Venice, became the privilege and the evidence of freedom."

"The spirit of the *Christian religion* would, before the discovery of America, have led to the entire abolition of the slave-trade, but for the hostility between the Christian Church and the followers of Mahomet. In the twelfth century, Pope Alexander III, true to the spirit of his office, which, during the supremacy of brute force in the middle ages, made of the chief minister of religion the tribune of the people and the guardian of the oppressed, had written, that '*Nature having made no slaves, all men have an equal right to liberty.*'"†

"The amelioration of the customs of Europe had proceeded from the influence of *religion*. It was the *clergy* who had broken up the Christian slave-markets at Bristol and at Hamburg, at Lyons and at Rome. At the epoch of the discovery of America, the moral opinion of the civilized world had abolished the traffic of Christian slaves; and was fast demanding the *emancipation of the serfs:* but bigotry had favoured a compromise with avarice; and the infidel was not yet included within the pale of humanity."‡

"The slave-trade between Africa and America was, I believe, never expressly sanctioned by the See of Rome. The spirit of the Roman Church was against it. Even Leo X, though his voluptuous life, making of his pontificate a continued carnival, might have deadened the sentiments of humanity and justice, declared, that '*not the Christian religion only, but nature herself, cries out against the state of slavery.*'"§

These few extracts are sufficient, I think, to prove that something more than "worldly causes" have contributed to remove

---

* History of the United States, I, 162.   † Ibid. 163.
‡ Ibid. 165.   § Ibid. 172.

slavery from European civilization. As long as Christianity exists upon the earth, and the consciences of its disciples are enlightened by the Spirit, a power will always be at work, higher than "worldly causes," tending to universal emancipation. Even these "worldly causes," to which allusion is made, are more or less controlled by the truth and influences of the Gospel.

6. I turn to another error, viz. : " It was not until the latter part of the eighteenth century that *a doubt* was expressed, on *either side of the Atlantic,* in relation to the perfect consistency of slavery with the precepts of the Gospel."

If I mistake not, the evidence, already adduced, will occasion very serious doubts in regard to the truth of the proposition, so far as it relates to the other side of the Atlantic. Let us, for the present, consider whether, on this side of the Atlantic, slavery and the Gospel were, always and everywhere, reckoned to be natural allies.

The Puritans did, it is true, consider themselves justified by the Old Testament in retaining Indian captives as bondsmen, according to the policy of the Israelites towards the Pagan nations. The Indian prisoners were few in number, and their case was a perplexing one. We do not justify Puritan reasoning on this subject; it was the reasoning of the day, both in Europe and in other parts of our own country. At that period, even white men were sold into slavery in Virginia. In the midst of such moral obtuseness, there were not wanting some signs of more correct views of human bondage, in New England. The following extracts are from Mr. Bancroft's history. The first paragraph relates to the sailing of the first vessel, owned in part by a member of the Church in Boston, to engage in the slave-trade.

"Throughout Massachusetts, the cry of justice was raised against the owners as malefactors and murderers. Richard Saltonstall felt himself moved by his duty as a magistrate, to denounce the act of stealing negroes as ' expressly contrary to the law of God and the law of the country ;' the guilty men were committed for the offence ; and, after advice with the elders, the representatives of the people, bearing ' witness against the heinous crimes of manstealing,' ordered *the negroes to be restored, at the public charge,* ' *to their own country,* with a letter expressing the indignation of the General Court' at their wrongs."[*] [This was in the year 1646.]

" When George Fox visited Barbadoes, in 1671, he enjoined it upon the planters, that they should ' deal mildly and gently with their negroes; and that after certain years of servitude, *they should make them free.*' The idea of George Fox had been anticipated by the fellow-citizens of Gorton and Roger Williams. Nearly twenty years had then elapsed since the representatives of Providence and Warwick, perceiving the disposition of people in the colony ' to buy negroes,' and hold them ' as slaves forever,' had enacted that no ' *black mankind,*' should, ' *by cove-*

* Bancroft's History, I, 174.

nant, bond, or otherwise,' be held to perpetual service; the master, ' at the end of ten years, shall set them free, as the manner is with English servants; and that man that will not let' his slave ' go free, or shall sell him away, to the end that he may be enslaved to others for a longer time, shall forfeit to the colony forty pounds. Now, forty pounds was nearly twice the value of a negro slave. The law was not enforced; but the principle lived among the people.' "*

" The thought of *general emancipation* early presented itself. Massachusetts, where the first planters assumed to themselves ' a right to treat the Indians on the foot of Canaanites and Amalekites,' was always opposed to the introduction of slaves from abroad; and in 1701, the town of Boston instructed its representatives, ' *to put a period to negroes being slaves.' "†*

It thus appears that, up to the beginning of the last century, there was a great deal of " doubt" in New England, in regard to " the perfect consistency of slavery with the precepts of the Gospel." Public opinion, however, seems to have afterwards relapsed into much indifference, until near the period of the Revolution, when Dr. Hopkins, of Newport, published a pamphlet on the " Slavery of the Africans, showing it to be the duty of the American Colonies to emancipate all the African slaves."‡ Dr. Hopkins apologizes for the want of conscience exhibited in New England by the " ignorance" of the owners of slaves; and " although this has been a very criminal ignorance, yet professors of religion, and real Christians, may have lived in this sin through an ignorance consistent with sincerity, and so as to be acceptable to God, through Jesus Christ, in their devotions," &c. Public attention now became much directed to slavery, both at the North and at the South.

The southern colonies had repeatedly remonstrated against the slave-trade. Judge Tucker, in his Notes on Blackstone, has collected a list of no less than twenty-three acts, passed by Virginia, having in view the repression of the importation of slaves. The motives were various, political as well as moral. In 1772, Virginia sent a petition to the throne, declaring, among other things, that " the importation of slaves into the colonies from the coast of Africa, hath *long* been considered a trade of *great inhumanity.*"

7. A very serious error in your letter, consists in attributing to *Infidelity* the awakened interest in Great Britain and the United States, in the suppression of the slave-trade and the abolition of slavery.

As if " worldly causes" were not low enough to account for the extinction of domestic servitude, Infidelity is summoned from the depths, as another ruling agent. This part of the solution of the question is your own, to which the instructions of Bishop Hopkins, allow me to say, naturally tended.

I ask your attention to the fact, that the period in which the

---

* Ibid. I, 174.   † Ibid. III, 408.   ‡ Published in 1776.

greatest masters of Infidelity were prominent actors, was the very period in which the slave-trade was carried on with the greatest energy, and the conscience of the whole world slumbered most profoundly over emancipation. From the year 1700, till the American Revolution, more negroes had been exported from Africa than ever before. During this interval, lived Shaftesbury, Bolingbroke, Hume, Voltaire, Rousseau, and the French Encyclopædists, great and small. Mr. Bancroft remarks, with his usual historical accuracy, "The philosophy of that day furnished to the African no protection against oppression." England, under the ministry of Bolingbroke, and his successors in office, openly advocated the slave-trade. It was a time of infidelity, of Arian and Deistical encroachment, and of ecclesiastical domination. It was a fit time for the climax of the slave-trade.

> " Loud and perpetual o'er the Atlantic waves,
> For guilty ages, rolled the tide of slaves;
> A tide that knew no fall, no turn, no rest—
> Constant as day and night, from East to West,
> Still wid'ning, deep'ning, swelling in its course,
> With boundless ruin and resistless force."

This state of active kidnapping in Africa, received its first check, not from Infidelity, but from the religion and patriotism of the confederated Colonies of North America. The delegates in Congress, without being specially empowered to do so, passed and promulgated, on the 6th of April, 1776, several months before the Declaration of Independence, a resolution that no slaves should be imported into the Confederation. Thus did Christianity and Liberty triumph over wickedness and crime.

The Northern States soon began to legislate in favour of emancipation. Under the impulses of a quickened sense of religious obligation, and of political consistency, slavery was undermined at the North. Much feeling also existed against the institution at the South, especially in Virginia, where the introduction of an Emancipation Act into the legislature was seriously contemplated, after the slave-trade was prohibited. It was *never* understood that Infidelity, as such, had any agency in these philanthropic measures throughout the country. Where religion failed to be prominent, patriotism supplied the motives of benevolent action. All the public documents of the day testify to the truth of this view of the subject.

The philanthropists of England, moved by equally pure and disinterested motives, aimed at the abolition of the slave-trade, simultaneously with their brethren in America. Granville Sharp, Wilberforce, Newton, Thornton, Scott, Macaulay, and their noble coadjutors, were among the foremost of the religious men of their age. Seldom, indeed, has Christianity claimed a higher triumph in the history of civilization, than when acts were passed for the abolition of the African slave-trade, and public measures were inaugurated for the abolition of slavery in America, and elsewhere. The religious world will be surprised to learn from Dr. Armstrong that Infidelity was the chief agent, whose culminating point was West Indian emancipation, under the auspices of England! Call West Indian emancipation a blunder, if you will—a political mistake, a social wrong, a moral imbecility—but hesitate, before the earnest philanthropy of Christian England, in behalf of injured Africa and the rights of mankind, is stigmatized with the taint of infidel inception and success.*

Your whole theory on this subject is utterly untenable. You might as well attempt to prove that the infidel philosophy on the subject of *civil government* had its culminating triumph in the formation of the *American Constitution*, as that the revived interest, in America and England, in the abolition of slavery, is indebted to the same low source for life and power. Washington, the representative man of his age, was a true representative of the Christianity and patriotism of his country, when in his last will and testament, he placed on record his views of the rights of mankind, and gave freedom to all his slaves.

8. Another historical error in your letter, is the declaration that good men, like Dr. Scott, have insidiously betrayed scriptural truth by erroneous expositions, and thus prepared the way for the most violent abolitionism.

I think, in the first place, that you do injustice to Dr. Scott by an erroneous "exposition" of his views. That able and judicious commentator does not say, or mean, that the Christian master should "greatly alleviate or nearly annihilate," any evil which concerns his *behaviour* "*to his servants.*" This is Dr. Armstrong's own "gloss." Dr. Scott says, that "Christian masters were instructed to behave towards their slaves in such a manner as would greatly alleviate, or nearly annihilate *the evils of slavery.*" The commentator well knew that, however exemplary might be the conduct of "Christian masters" towards their own slaves, on their own plantations, some of the "evils of slavery," as a system, would still remain in existence.

If Dr. Scott, in his other remarks, intended to express the opinion that the Apostles considered slavery to be in itself sinful, but were restrained by prudential considerations from enjoining emancipation, he was certainly wrong. It is probable that he merely intended to vindicate, on general principles, the true scriptural plan. However that may be, he was correct, when he added that "the principles of both the law and the Gospel, when carried to their consequences, will infallibly abolish slavery." Was he not authorized, in expounding Scripture, to give what he conceived to be the full meaning of the passage? Dr. Hodge, in like manner, says in his commentary on Ephesians, 6 : 5, "The scriptural doc-

---

* For one, I have not yet lost all confidence in the wisdom of this measure.

trine is opposed to the opinion that slavery is in itself a desirable institution, and as such to be cherished and perpetuated."

Mr. Barnes's remarks, which you quote, I agree with you in repudiating. But he is as far from being an infidel as Dr. Scott. If Mr. Barnes goes a " bowshot beyond Dr. Scott," I think that, in regard to the connivance of either with Infidelity, you draw a bow " at a venture."

Dr. Scott's commentaries were published in 1796. They have certainly had little influence in imposing Anti-slavery opinions upon the Presbyterian Church. As far back as 1787, our highest judicatory uttered stronger declarations than are to be found in those commentaries. The Synod declared that it " highly approved of the general principles in favour of *universal liberty* that prevail in America, and the interest which many of the States have taken in *promoting the abolition of slavery.*"

Commentators, from the days of Dr. Scott, onward, naturally noticed the subject of slavery in its relation to Scripture, more than their predecessors. So far as their commentaries are erroneous, they are to be condemned. Each is to be judged by himself. I do not believe in the philosophical or infidel succession you have attempted to establish.

9. A *brief sketch of ultra Pro-slavery opinions* may be fairly given as an offset to the Anti-slavery history of your Letter.

Previous to the formation of the American Constitution, public opinion, in this country, had been gathering strength, adversely to the slave-trade and slavery. The first legislature of the State of Virginia prohibited the importation of Africans ; and some of her most distinguished public men were unfavourable, not only to the increase, but even to the continuance of slavery within her borders. The Congress of the old Confederation, with the unanimous consent of all the Southern as well as Northern States, provided, in 1787, that slavery should be forever excluded from the Northwest Territory, which territory then constituted the whole of the public domain. In the same year, the framers of the Constitution of the United States enacted that the African slave-trade should cease in 1808, so far as the " existing States" were concerned ; reserving to Congress the right to prohibit it before that time in new States or Territories—a right which Congress exercised in 1804, by prohibiting the importation of Africans into the new Territory of Orleans.

Daniel Webster, in the Senate of the United States, affirmed that two things " are quite clear as historical truths. One is, that there was an expectation that, on the ceasing of the importation of slaves from Africa, slavery would begin to run out here. That was hoped and expected. Another is, that as far as there was any power in Congress to prevent the spread of slavery in the United States, that power was executed in the most absolute manner, and to the fullest extent. . . . . But opinion has changed —greatly changed—changed North and changed South. Slavery is not regarded, at the South now, as it was then."* Without carrying this sketch into the details of modern party politics, which would be foreign to my purpose, it is sufficient to note that this change of sentiment, at the South, has grown more and more marked, down to the present time. Even the project of *reviving the African slave-trade* has been recently entertained in the legislatures of several States. Slavery is now publicly advocated as a desirable and permanent institution, having a complete justification in the word of God. Its advocacy is, by others, placed on the infidel ground of the original diversity of races. In fact, is not Infidelity as busily engaged in vindicating, and propping up, ultra pro-slavery opinions at the South, as it has ever been in agitating its untruths, at the North?† There is little religion in either extreme. It is to be hoped that the tendency on both sides of the question to a change from bad to worse, will be arrested in the good providence of God.

10. Your historical sketch errs in *reducing all opposition to slavery into the same category.*

A history of Anti-slavery opinions requires careful discrimination, in order to do justice to all parties. The "conservatives" differ fundamentally from the ultra faction, which denounces slaveholding as necessarily sinful, and which accepts no solution but immediate and universal emancipation. Nor do they, or can they, sympathize with the equally fanatical opinions on the other side. We profess to maintain the firm, scriptural ground, occupied by our Church from the beginning. Presbyterians at the North have been enabled, under God, to uphold the testimonies of the General Assembly in their incorrupt integrity. Will not our brethren at the South appreciate our position, and the service we have rendered to morals and religion? Your historical sketch confounds all varieties of opinion in opposition to the permanence of slavery, and reduces them to one common principle of evil. Omission, under such circumstances, is commission. It inflicts an injury upon your truest friends; and more, it disparages the cause of truth and righteousness. Far be it from me to impute to you any intention of this kind. On the contrary, I am sure that you will gladly rectify the inadvertence.

I rejoice in the belief that the Presbyterian Church is substantially united on the fundamental principles involved in this question. If any danger should hereafter threaten our unity, it will arise from the extreme advocates of slavery. So far as I have any personal knowledge of my brethren in the Southern section of

---

* Mr. Webster emphatically stated, in the same speech, that, at the formation of the Constitution, "there was, if not an entire unanimity of sentiment, a general concurrence of sentiment running through *the whole community,* and especially entertained by the *eminent men of all parts of the country,*" on this subject.

† It is well known, that the infidel publication of Gliddon and Agassiz, one of whose principal aims is to prove that the negro is not a descendant of Adam, has had an extensive circulation in the Southern States.

the Church, or have observed their proceedings in the General Assembly, I have yet to learn that they are disposed to depart from our ancient Presbyterian testimonies. Few persons, on either side, seem inclined to adopt extreme opinions. Various statements in your Letters have excited, perhaps unreasonably, the apprehension of a tendency in them to create and cherish divisions. One of the impressions, derived from the perusal of your third Letter, is that slavery is fortified by the Bible and the Church, and that the institution would be safe enough in perpetuity, if "worldly causes" would keep in the right direction, and Infidelity cease its assaults. Your historical account is, at least, so apologetical, that it may conciliate, and even stimulate, the ultra defenders of slavery.

You rightly suggest that error has an insidious beginning. It is on this principle, doubtless, that ultra men at the North, and at the South, have succeeded in accomplishing much injury. The "classic story" of the fall of Troy, by means of the wooden horse filled with Grecian enemies, affords an instructive lesson. The enemies without the city would have built that structure in vain, if leaders within the city had not brought it through the walls. It is through the breaches, made by Christian chieftains, that Infidelity is drawn into our citadel. Extreme views, on either side, combine to overthrow the true doctrine of the Church.

It may be affirmed, without boasting, and in humble gratitude to God, that the Presbyterian Church occupies a commanding position, at the present time, among the hosts of God's elect. Our declared principles on slavery, emancipation, and Christian fellowship will endure the scrutiny, and at last command the admiration of the world. Unterrified by Northern fanaticism, and unseduced by Southern, Presbyterians behold their banner floating peacefully over their ancient ramparts. With continued UNITY in our councils, the cause of philanthropy and religion will, under God, be safe in our charge, and be handed down with increasing victories, from generation to generation.

I am yours fraternally,
C. VAN RENSSELAER.

Rejoinders.

DR. ARMSTRONG'S FIRST REJOINDER.

ON THE SCRIPTURE DOCTRINE OF SLAVERY.

To the Rev. C. Van Rensselaer, D.D.:

In its first settlement by the white man, Kentucky was so often the scene of savage warfare as to have received the name of "the dark and bloody ground." The hardy pioneer as he scaled its mountains, wound along by the side of its rivers, or penetrated its forests, proceeded with wary step and slow, rifle in hand, and ready for instant conflict. Many a time has the motion caused by the winds of heaven, been thought to mark the presence of some lurking foe; and many a time has the rifle-shot dissipated the traveller's fears, though it took no life. None but the fool would consider it an impeachment of the traveller's courage that he moved with caution, nor of his wisdom, that he sometimes shot at the wind.

The "slavery discussion" well deserves the title of "the dark and bloody ground" of modern polemics; the tomahawk and scalping-knife are fit symbols of the weapons often used, whilst the "shriek for freedom," not unlike the Indian war-whoop, has lent its maddening influence to the fight.

Aware of this, I am not surprised to find you, in your "Conservative Replies," charging upon me opinions which I do not entertain, and which—I write it after carefully reading over all I have published on the subject—I have not expressed. And you will not understand me as intending to impeach either your intelligence or your candour, when I add, you seem to me to have misapprehended the scope of my argument, and the position I have assumed, both in my "Christian Doctrine of Slavery" and in my "Letters," subsequently addressed to yourself. And lest you should think that, like the lawyers of old, "I am lading you with a burden, grievous to be borne, whilst I touch it not with one of my fingers," I will couple this charge with a confession,—I certainly misapprehended the position you intended to assume in the brief "book notice," which has given rise to this discussion—but of this, more hereafter.

To guard against misapprehension, in what I now write, I shall make use of division into sections, and all such other appliances as are calculated to secure perspicuity.

§ 1. *True sense of the expression, "the Christian doctrine of slavery."*

In a thorough examination of domestic slavery, some of the questions which claim consideration are *religious* questions, others are *political*. The *whole* doctrine of slavery is, in part, a *Christian* doctrine, which falls properly within the province of the Church, to be determined, taught, and enforced with her spiritual sanctions; and in part, a *political* doctrine, which it is the business of the statesman to expound, and the civil ruler to apply, in the exercise of the authority which by God's ordinance belongs to them. In this, we fully agree.

In attempting to draw the distinction between the Christian and the Political, let us substitute for the case of Domestic Slavery that of Civil Despotism. We both agree that the Bible places the two in the same category. There will, therefore, be no danger of being betrayed into error by the substitution, and we will thus be enabled to approach the subject in a way in which we will be less likely to be influenced by prejudice than if we approached it directly.

I would make a statement in brief of the *whole* doctrine of Civil Despotism in some such terms as these,—and if you substitute Domestic Slavery for Civil Despotism in each several proposition, as you pass along, you will have my faith with respect to it also.

1. Civil Despotism belongs "in morals to the *adiaphora*, to things indifferent. It is expedient or inexpedient, right or wrong, according to circumstances."

2. As compared with other forms of civil government, " in this present evil world," it belongs to a lower state of Christian civilization in the subject, than limited monarchy or republicanism.

3. The question of its continuance in any particular instance, should be determined by the consideration of "well-being" "or the general good."

4. So long as Civil Despotism lawfully continues among any people, the Christian subject is bound to obedience; and, the Church is bound to respect the institution, and to instruct the people in their duties, as those duties are set forth in the word of God.

To this statement, in its several particulars, I do not think that you will object.

How much of this doctrine is *Christian*, as contradistinguished from *Political*, and therefore falls properly within the province of the Church to teach and enforce ?

I answer. Just so much of it as is taught in the word of God, and no more. In this, as in all similar cases, a part of the truth is taught us in the word of God; another part, we learn in the use of that reason which God has given for our guidance in such matters. The latter will never be inconsistent with the former ; though it will be in addition to it, and therefore, distinct from it.

The question then—How much of this doctrine is properly *Christian ?* resolves itself into this other—How much of this doctrine is distinctly taught us in the word of God ? To this, I reply—

1. The word of God teaches that so long as a despotic government lawfully continues among any people, rulers and subjects alike are bound to discharge the duties belonging to their several stations, and the Church is bound to respect the institution, and by her teaching and discipline to enforce the discharge of duty, as that duty is set forth in the word of God.

2. The word of God teaches that despotism is not a sinful form

of government, and is not to be treated as an "offence" by the Church.

Does any one object to the terms in which the second proposition is stated? My reply is—This is just the truth, both as to substance and form, presented us in the word of God. "Let every soul be subject unto the higher powers. For there is no power but of God: the powers that be are ordained of God. Whosoever, therefore, resisteth the power, resisteth the ordinance of God; and they that resist shall receive to themselves damnation." (Rom. 13 : 1–4.) For an admirable exposition of this passage, see Dr. Hodge's Commentary.

Does any one ask how is this statement to be reconciled with that already made, when setting forth what I received as the *whole* doctrine of civil despotism? My reply is—I see no discrepancy between them. The one statement is more comprehensive than the other, and fairly includes it.

When I write, "Civil despotism is expedient or inexpedient, *right* or *wrong*, according to circumstances,"—I do not mean *wrong* in the proper sense of *sinful*. Should any Christian man, at the present day, avow the belief that a despotic government would better secure "the general good" of our people, than the form of government under which we live—and I have heard such an opinion avowed more than once—I should controvert his opinion as wrong, but I should not denounce him as a sinner for holding it. Should he, in any lawful manner, lawful under God's law, attempt to replace our republican by a despotic government, I should resist him, in my character of a citizen; but I have no authority to treat him as an *offender*, in my character of a ruler in the Church. But should any Christian man "resist," in the sense in which Paul uses that word, in Rom. 13 : 2, our republican government, and more especially if he taught others so to do, I should at once charge him with sin, and treat him as an "offender."

When I write, "Civil despotism is not a sinful form of government," the idea that where such a government exists, it must of right always continue, is no more implied, than the doctrine of "passive obedience" is implied in Paul's words, written when Nero was emperor, "Whosoever, therefore, resisteth the power, resisteth the ordinance of God; and they that resist shall receive to themselves damnation." Or the doctrine of "the divine right of kings," is implied in Peter's words, "Submit yourselves to every ordinance of man for the Lord's sake; whether it be to the king as supreme, or unto governors, as unto them that are sent by him for the punishment of evil-doers, and for the praise of them that do well."

In interpreting the language of Scripture, or the language used in setting forth the *Scripture* or *Christian* doctrine, on such a subject as this, we must bear in mind the admitted truth, that the Scriptures were given to teach us religion and not politics; and all that needs to be shown, respecting any political right or doctrine, commended to us as true by reason, is, that it is not in conflict with the word of God. The "right of revolution," *i. e.*, the right of a people to change their form of government, is a political right—the doctrine of revolution is a political doctrine; and, therefore, we have no reason to expect that they will be taught us in the word of God. I receive them as true, upon the authority of reason. Receiving them upon this authority, it is enough for me, it is all that I have a right to expect, that it shall be clear ; and I think that it is clear that the Scriptures teach nothing at variance with them.

Does any one ask, why insist upon the statement " Civil despotism is not a sinful form of government, and is not to be treated as an 'offence' by the Church," when I admit the truth of the other, " Civil Despotism belongs, in morals, to the *adiaphora*, to things indifferent ; it is expedient or inexpedient, right or wrong, according to circumstances ?" I answer—Because I am professing to give a statement of the Christian or Scriptural doctrine, *i. e.*, what the word of God teaches, respecting civil despotism. The first statement does this; the latter does more than this. The first statement sets forth truth which must bind the conscience, and exactly defines the limits of the Church's power. The latter, though I receive it as all true, does neither the one nor the other.

As already intimated, if you will substitute domestic slavery for civil despotism throughout this section, you will have a statement of what I believe respecting that subject. In my book, " The Christian Doctrine of Slavery," I have written, " Throughout, the author has kept these two ends in view. 1. A faithful exhibition of the doctrine respecting slavery taught by Christ and his Apostles. Nothing which they taught has been intentionally omitted. No topic which they omitted—however essential to a full discussion of slavery as a civil and political question, it may be—has been introduced ;" and when stating the question to be discussed, I stated it in these terms, " What do Christ and his Apostles—commissioned by him to complete the sacred canon, and perfect the organization of the Church—teach respecting slavery, and the relation in which the Church stands to that institution ?" (See p. 8.) The reply given to this question—" They teach that slaveholding is not a sin in the sight of God, and is not to be accounted an ' offence' by his church" (see p. 8), &c., is, I yet think, the correct reply ; and after examining your principal objections to it, I will briefly state some additional reasons for thinking so.

§ 2. *Statement of the difference between us.*

In your first letter you write, " I now proceed to the subject of your first letter, viz. : the proper statement of the *scriptural doctrine* of slavery."

" Your statement is, ' slaveholding is not a sin in the sight of God, and is not to be accounted an offence by his church.' "

" My statement is, ' slaveholding is not necessarily and in all circumstances sinful.' "

Simply calling your attention to the fact that it is " THE SCRIP-

TURAL DOCTRINE," i. e., what the word of God teaches respecting slavery, for which we are seeking a brief expression, in general terms—I accept your statement of the difference between us.

§ 3. *The General Assembly's paper of* 1845.

The correctness of your "form of statement" you think confirmed by the coincidence with the testimonies of the Presbyterian Church—while of mine, you write, " whatever added explanations may cause it to approximate to the language of the General Assembly, the naked words are as dissimilar, as a leafless tree is from one of living green."

In proof of this you make the following five quotations from the paper adopted by the General Assembly in 1845, viz. :

1. " The question, which is now unhappily agitating and dividing other branches of the Church, is, whether the holding of slaves is under all circumstances, a heinous sin, calling for the discipline of the Church."

2. " The question which this Assembly is called upon to decide is this: Do the Scriptures teach that the holding of slaves, without regard to circumstances, is a sin ?"

3. " The Apostles did not denounce the relation itself as sinful."

4. " The Assembly cannot denounce the holding of slaves as necessarily a heinous and scandalous sin."

5. " The existence of domestic slavery, under the circumstances in which it is found in the southern portion of the country, is no bar to Christian communion."

Such are your quotations. Did it escape your notice, my good brother, that the first two of your quotations are not deliverances of the Assembly, but simply statements of what Abolitionists were contending for in other churches, and what certain Abolition memorialists had demanded of them ; and that the second two, are the answers of the Assembly to this demand—where the answer naturally and properly takes its form from that of the demand to which it is an answer. This, which appears upon the face of the quotations, is placed beyond all doubt when we turn to the paper adopted by the Assembly, and examine them in the connection in which they occur. In so far, then, as these quotations are relied upon as authority for "language" or "a form of expression," it is the authority of the Abolitionists, and not of the Assembly, which they afford ; an authority of which we may say, as has been said of poor land, " the more a man has of it, the worse he is off."

Your last quotation, is a proper deliverance of the Assembly. It is a part of the first of the two resolutions with which the paper adopted by the Assembly closes—resolutions, in which that venerable body give a summary of the principles before stated in a practical form, i. e., as in their judgment, those principles apply to slaveholding " in the southern portion of our country." But the authority of that quotation is, I think, clearly on my side and not on yours;—certain I am, if you had written, slaveholding "in the circumstances in which it exists in the southern portion of our country" is not sinful, I should never have thought of objecting to your statement.

The deliverance, in general terms, of the Assembly of 1845, is in these words, "The Assembly intend simply to say, that since Christ and his inspired Apostles did not make the holding of slaves a bar to communion, we, as a court of Christ, have no authority to do so ; since they did not attempt to remove it from the Church by legislation, we have no authority to legislate on the subject," &c. This deliverance is a scriptural one, and covers all the ground that my "statement," fairly interpreted, does.

§ 4. *Dr. Hodge's Essay.*

You make certain quotations from Dr. Hodge's celebrated article on Slavery—one of the ablest articles which has appeared on this subject, and an article which claims particular attention from the connection in which it stands, as a matter of history, with the position of the Presbyterian Church, O. S., in which he adopts a "form of expression" similar to yours, viz.:

(1.) "An equally obvious deduction is, that slaveholding is not necessarily sinful."

(2.) "Both political despotism and domestic slavery belong in morals to the *adiaphora*, to things indifferent. They may be expedient or inexpedient, right or wrong, according to circumstances. Belonging to the same class, they should be treated in the same way. Neither is to be denounced as necessarily sinful, and to be abolished immediately under all circumstances."

(3.) "Slavery is a question of circumstances, and not a *malum in se.*" "Simply to prove that slaveholding interferes with natural rights, is not enough to justify the conclusion that it is necessarily and universally sinful."

(4.) "These forms of society are not necessarily, or in themselves, just or unjust; but become one or the other according to circumstances."

(5.) "Monarchy, aristocracy, democracy, domestic slavery, are right or wrong, as they are for the time being conducive to this great end, or the reverse."

(6.) "We have ever maintained that slaveholding is not in itself sinful; that the right to personal liberty is conditioned by the ability to exercise beneficially that right."

(7.) "Nothing can be more distinct than the right to hold slaves in certain circumstances, and the right to render slavery perpetual."

In these quotations, I cheerfully grant, that the language of Dr. Hodge is similar to yours. But then, I must ask you to notice,

1. In several of them he is, obviously, meeting the arguments and assailing the positions of the Abolitionists, and his statements naturally and properly take their form from those of his opponents, and,

2. In others, he is stating the doctrine of slavery, as it presents

itself when deduced from general principles, *i. e.*, he is stating the *whole* doctrine of slavery, without attempting to distinguish between the *scriptural* and the *political* in that doctrine. Fairly interpreted, there is nothing in any of these statements quoted by you, from which I have any disposition to dissent.

But listen to Dr. Hodge, as he states the doctrine of slavery directly deducible from the word of God,—and I quote from the same essay.

(1.) "When Southern Christians are told that they are guilty of a heinous crime, worse than piracy, robbery, or murder, because they hold slaves, when they know that *Christ and his Apostles never denounced slaveholding as a crime, never called upon men to renounce it as a condition of admission into the Church,* they are shocked and offended, without being convinced." (Hodge's Essays and Reviews, p. 484.)

(2.) "Our argument from this acknowledged fact is, that if God allowed slavery to exist, if he directed how slaves might be lawfully acquired, and how they were to be treated, *it is vain to contend that slaveholding is a sin, and yet profess reverence for the Scriptures.*" (p. 492.)

(3.) "As it appears to us too clear to admit of either denial or doubt, that *the Scriptures do sanction slaveholding;* that under the old dispensation it was expressly permitted by divine command, and under the New Testament is nowhere forbidden or denounced; but, on the contrary, *acknowledged to be consistent with the Christian character and profession (that is, consistent with justice, mercy, holiness, love to God and love to man), to declare it to be a heinous crime, is a direct impeachment of the word of God.*" (p. 503.)

If the language of Dr. Hodge, in the quotations which you have made, gives countenance to your "form of expression," does not his language in those which I have made, give equally distinct countenance to mine? And notice, here—

(1.) My quotations are exactly "in point," since they cover the precise question respecting an expression for the *Scriptural* doctrine of slavery—whilst yours are not "in point."

(2.) Dr. Hodge uses this language without intending to teach, or being thought to teach "the permanence of slavery, as an ordinance of God, on a level with marriage or civil government." (Dr. Van Rensselaer's Sec. Let.)

(3.) The Essay of Dr. Hodge, from which these quotations are made, together with Dr. Baxter's "Essay on the Abolition of Slavery," published the same year (1836), stand in intimate historic connection with the position respecting slavery assumed by the Presbyterian Church, Old School, in its separation from the New. Beyond all question, they had more to do in determining that position than any other papers or speeches whatsoever. Why then should my "language" sound "like an old tune with *unpleasant alterations*" (Dr. Van Rensselaer's First Letter), when it is precisely similar to that used by them, at that time?

§ 5. "*A weapon to do battle with.*"

You object to my statement because, you think, "as a weapon to do battle with, it invites assault without the power to repel. It lacks the Scriptural characteristic of fighting a good fight. It carries with it no available and victorious force."

If this *opinion* of yours be well-founded, it expresses a very serious objection to my "form of expression." The great conflict of the Church of God, in our country and our day, is her conflict with Abolitionism; and it becomes her to arm herself with weapons which will not disappoint her in the hour of trial.

As an offset to your *opinion*, let me state a *fact*, in part known to the public already, through another channel; and let me say with Paul, if I seem to have "become a fool in glorying, ye have compelled me."

In the Presbyterian Herald, May 7th, 1857, the editor, after stating, at some length, his reasons for such a course, writes— "We wrote a letter, last winter, to Rev. Mr. Dexter, the leading editor of one of their papers at Boston, The Congregationalist, proposing to him to choose one of his brethren, in whose candour, ability, learning, and Christian temper, he had confidence, and we would select an Old School Presbyterian minister of the same character, and let the two discuss, in our respective columns, the question whether the New Testament teaches that slaveholding should be made a term of communion in Christ's Church, or, in other words, whether it teaches that it is inconsistent with Christian character to hold slaves; the articles of each writer to be published simultaneously in the two papers, and afterwards in book form, under the joint supervision of the editors of the two papers. To this letter we received a very kind and courteous reply, accepting our proposition conditionally. We named the Rev. George D. Armstrong, D.D., pastor of the Presbyterian Church, in Norfolk, Virginia, as our selection; and requested the Rev. Mr. Dexter to select some New England man of equal standing, and put the correspondence as to the precise question to be discussed, into their hands. Without going into further details, we will only add, that the negotiations for a discussion have failed, for the present at least; and Dr. Armstrong has prepared a small work for the press, entitled 'The Christian Doctrine of Slavery.' After the issue of the work, the proposed discussion of its positions may yet take place in the columns of the Herald and Congregationalist." Thus much writes Dr. Hill.

I will now add, that "the negotiations for a discussion failed," because we could not agree upon such a statement of the question to be discussed, as seemed fair to both parties. When this result became evident, I made the proposition to publish my argument— as I subsequently did; and then, to make this published argument the starting-point for a discussion, in the form of review and rejoinder; the terms, in other respects, remaining as before. To the fairness of this proposition, no objection was made. As soon as printed, two copies were sent to the other party. And, although a year has now elapsed, neither Dr. Hill nor I have heard anything of the proposed discussion from that day to this.

Such is my *fact*, which, pardon me for saying it, does not agree very well with your *opinion*. And I am sure you will not say, as was once said by a good man, who shall be nameless, in circumstances somewhat similar, "so much the worse for the fact then."

§ 7. *Objections to Dr. Van Rensselaer's statement.*

In my "first letter" I stated two objections to your "form of statement," both of which you seem to have misapprehended. I must, therefore, restate them, and add some further explanation.

"1. It is an unusual form of stating ethical propositions such as this, and though it is broad enough to acquit the slaveholding member of the Church, it gives to his acquittal a sort of 'whip, and clear him air,'—pardon my use of this homely expression; I can find no other which will so well convey the exact idea I wish to give utterance to—which seems to me in contrast with all the New Testament deliverances on the subject."

A "whip, and clear him" verdict, is a verdict given by a jury, when they believe a prisoner guilty, though his guilt cannot be proven; and being compelled by the evidence to acquit him, they yet award him a flogging, on the score of their belief of his bad character in general; and does not mean, as you have interpreted the phrase, "strike first, and then acquit."

God's people, whose lot in his providence has been cast in the midst of slavery, have not only weighty responsibilities, and responsibilities to be met in the midst of many difficulties, arising out of their connection with that institution, but they have had much to bear from their Christian brethren in other parts of our country, in the twenty-five years last past. Misapprehension and personal abuse are the least of their wrongs. To be told, as they have been, even at the table of our common Lord, "Stand aside, for I am holier than thou," they might well have borne, comforted by the assurance that though man might condemn them, "the Lord of glory" would not. But the worst of their wrong is, they have been constantly hindered in doing "God's work in God's way," with respect to the slave race among them, by men "desiring to be teachers of the law, but understanding neither what they say, nor whereof they affirm."

Do not think that I mean to class you among this number. I know well that your views and your uniform course of conduct have been very different from theirs. But I object to your "form of expressing" the Scripture doctrine of slavery, because your language does seem to countenance such views as theirs; and, in this particular, is in contrast with the language uniformly used by inspired Apostles when treating of this subject. Let Dr. Barnes specify the "*circumstances*," and I doubt whether even he would object to your statement—"Slaveholding is not necessarily and in all *circumstances* sinful." At any rate, he distinctly admits that Abraham's slaveholding was no sin.

2. But my principal objection to your "form of expression," as .a statement of *the Scripture doctrine of slavery*, is that which, in my first letter, I set forth in the words: " *When taken apart from all explanations, it does not fairly cover all the ground which the doctrine of Christ and his inspired Apostles covers.*"

The argument on this point, embodied in the Assembly's paper of '45, and that of Dr. Hodge's Essay, is substantially the same with that which I have presented, more in detail, in my " Christian Doctrine of Slavery." Let us look at this argument, and see just what ground it does fairly cover.

(1.) The Assembly of '45 say—" Since Christ and his inspired Apostles did not make the holding of slaves a bar to communion, we, as a court of Christ, have no authority to do so."

Give this argument, now, the form of a syllogism, that we may examine it the more carefully :

A. Whatever Christ and his inspired Apostles refused to make a bar to communion, a court of Christ has no authority to make such.

But, Christ and his inspired Apostles did refuse to make slaveholding a bar to communion.

Therefore, a court of Christ has no authority to make slaveholding a bar to communion.

(2.) The Assembly add—"Since they," *i. e.*, Christ and his inspired Apostles, " did not attempt to remove it from the Church by legislation, we have no authority to legislate on the subject."

Give this, also, the form of a syllogism :

B. Whatever Christ and his inspired Apostles did not attempt to legislate out of the Church, the Church has no authority to remove by legislation.

But, Christ and his inspired Apostles did not attempt to legislate slaveholding out of the Church.

Therefore, the Church has no authority to remove slaveholding from her body by legislation.

Dr. Hodge writes, as quoted in Sec. 4, " As it appears·to us too clear to admit of either denial or doubt, that *the Scriptures do sanction slaveholding; that under the old dispensation it was expressly permitted by divine command, and under the New Testament is nowhere forbidden or denounced, but, on the contrary, acknowledged to be consistent with the Christian character and profession (that is, consistent with justice, mercy, holiness, love to God, and love to man), to declare it to be a heinous crime, is a direct impeachment of the word of God.*"

Give this the form of a syllogism :

C. To declare that to be a sin which, under the old dispensation, was expressly permitted by divine command, and, under the New Testament, is nowhere forbidden or denounced, but, on the contrary, acknowledged to be consistent with the Christian character and profession (that is, consistent with justice, mercy, holiness, love to God, and love to man), is a direct impeachment of the word of God.

But slaveholding, under the old dispensation, was expressly permitted, and under the New Testament, was acknowledged to be consistent with the Christian character and profession, &c.

Therefore, to declare slaveholding a sin is a direct impeachment of the word of God.

Now, notice—(1.) The major premise in each of these three syllogisms, is a statement of a principle, in its nature unchangeable; in fact, just the "VII" of the "preliminary principles," in the "Form of Government of the Presbyterian Church,"—"That all Church power, whether exercised by the body in general, or in the way of representation by delegated authority, is only *ministerial and declarative;* that is to say, that the Holy Scriptures are the only rule of faith and manners; that no Church judicatory ought to pretend to make laws to bind the conscience in virtue of their own authority; and that all their decisions should be founded upon the revealed will of God."

(2.) The minor premise in each is a statement of fact, which, if it be a true statement, must always continue such.

Whatever then the argument expressed in these syllogisms proves, it proves not for this or that age, but for *all time*, until Christ shall come the second time and bring to a close the present dispensation.

If the argument in syllogism A, proved that the Church had "no authority to make slaveholding a bar to communion" in 1845, it proves that the Church never will have such authority.

If the argument in syllogism B, proves that the Church had "no authority to legislate slaveholding out of itself" in 1845, it proves that she never will have such authority.

If the argument in syllogism C, proved that "to declare slaveholding a sin was a direct impeachment of the word of God" in 1837, it must prove the same now, and will prove the same until we get a new word of God as our rule of faith.

As already remarked, the argument presented in these syllogisms is the same in substance, which I have presented more in detail, in my "Christian Doctrine of Slavery."

Is this argument a sound one? Are the premises fairly stated?

If you answer YES—Then, I say, nothing can be more clear than that your statement, "slaveholding is not necessarily and in all *circumstances* sinful," "does not fairly cover all the ground which the doctrine of Christ and his inspired Apostles covers." There are no "*circumstances*" introduced into the premises, and hence, according to a fundamental principle of logic, none can be introduced into the conclusion. It is true, that taken in connection with your "explanation," that you do not wish to see our Church depart from "the scriptural position" which she has assumed, it does practically, for the present, cover that ground,—but no statement short of what you term my "too broad conclusion" will fully and fairly cover that ground.

If you answer No—Then, I say, point out distinctly, where the fallacy in the argument is. If "*circumstances*" ought to have been introduced into the premises—state, distinctly (1) in which premise, and (2) what the "*circumstances*" are. Meet the argument "fairly and squarely," for thus only can you influence the opinions of thinking men. To help you in this, is one object I have had in view, in giving to the argument the logical form of the syllogism.

For myself, I believe the argument is a sound one; I believe the premises are fairly and fully stated; and, therefore, I find myself shut up to the conclusion, that "slaveholding is not a sin in the sight of God, and is not to be accounted an offence by his Church." And I feel myself confirmed in this judgment, by the fact that the General Assembly, and Dr. Hodge, when they attempt to state the Scripture premises, state them, substantially, as I do.

Of this I am certain. The prejudices of my early life and education have not helped me forward towards the conclusion I have reached. Their influence was all the other way. Of this, also, I am certain. My political opinions have not helped me. Their influence, too, has been all the other way. And I think I can add, my interest has not swayed me. I am not a slaveholder—though Dr. McMaster does name me among the "slave-driving hierarchs" of the South. I never have been a slaveholder. And if I am labouring in the cause of Christ, at the South, to-day, it is not because inviting fields of labour in the Free States have not been offered me. If I know anything of the history of my opinions on this subject, they are opinions which have been formed under the influence of a careful and prayerful study of God's word. And let me here add, that I believe, where our Northern brethren have spent *one* hour in the careful and prayerful study of what God's word teaches on the subject of slavery, we, of the South, have spent *ten*. And this ought to be so, for upon us, in God's providence, the immediate responsibility with respect to slavery rests.

Near the close of your Second Letter, you ask,—" Are there no eternal principles of justice, no standard of human rights, by which a system of servitude shall submit to be judged, and in whose presence it shall be made to plead for justification?" I answer, Yes, my good brother, there are eternal principles of justice, there is a standard of human rights;—and I add, there is a Judge too, who "sitteth at the top of judgment," whose very "foolishness is wiser than the wisdom of man;" by whom those "eternal principles of justice," and this "standard of human rights" have been applied to the very case before us. His decision is "of record." And having this decision, we will never consent to have the case appealed to any lower tribunal.

§ 8. *What my statement does not include.*

Knowing how difficult a matter it is to do an opponent justice on this "dark and bloody ground" of modern polemics, even when our purposes are most fair—and I do not question that yours are such—let me in concluding this letter, state distinctly, certain things which, I think, are neither included nor implied in the statement of the Christian doctrine of slavery for which I am contending.

1. It does not imply *a sanction of the incidental evils, attaching to slavery in Paul's day, or as it exists now.*

The word of God did not teach then, nor does it teach now, that the master may sinlessly withhold from his slave "kind treatment," or "adequate compensation for service," or perpetuate "his ignorance and debasement."

As I shall have to speak of this subject more fully in my next letter, I content myself, for the present, with remarking, that the only slavery which the Bible justifies now, or ever did justify, is a slavery which "is a condition of mutual rights and obligations, the right of the master being to receive obedience and service, the right of the slave to receive that which is just and equal." (Chn. Doc. Slav. p. 105.)

This, if I mistake not, is just what you and Dr. Spring, as quoted by you, most improperly call "*apprenticeship.*" The difference between slavery and apprenticeship, is not a difference in the degree of rigor with which one is made to serve. The peculiarity of apprenticeship, as both the use and the etymology of the term determine —(see Webster's Dictionary)—is, that the service is rendered with an eye to instruction in some art or calling; and with no sort of propriety can the service authorized by Moses' law, either that of the Jew or the Gentile, be called an apprenticeship; since it was not a servitude authorized or entered into with any such view as this.

And, whilst speaking of this misuse of terms, let me refer to another, viz., "Slavery in itself considered." What is the proper meaning of that expression? I should answer—slavery, distinct from the incidental evils which may attach to it in any particular age or country; and, thus understood, the formula, "Slaveholding, in itself considered, is not sinful," would be perfectly satisfactory to me—would cover all the ground which I think the word of God covers. But, most unfortunately, modern usage, especially the usage of writers in the slavery controversy, has attached a different meaning to the phrase, a meaning which you have correctly set forth in your First Letter—"Slaveholding, in itself considered, is not sinful; that is to say, it is not a *malum in se;* or, in other words, *it is a relation which may be justified by circumstances.*" For this reason, and this alone, I did not use this formula in my "Christian Doctrine of Slavery," and cannot accept it now.

2. It does not imply that "the citizen in the Free States can

always *lawfully* enter into this relation" (*i. e.*, the relation of a slaveholder), "when he removes into a State where the laws do sanction slavery;" if by "*lawfully,*" you mean without sin!

The case, as stated by yourself, is a case concerning, not sin as attaching to an institution, but sin as attaching to the conduct of the individual man; a case which is fully discussed by Paul, in the 14th chapter of Romans. If there be "tens of thousands of Christians in the Free States, who could not enter voluntarily into this relation without involving their conscience in sin," then I say with Paul—"To him that esteemeth anything to be unclean, to him it is unclean," but "why is my liberty judged of another man's conscience?"

3. It does not imply "*the permanence of slavery, as an ordinance of God, on a level with marriage or civil government.*"

The reasoning which would educe such a conclusion from the deliverances of the word of God, on the subject of slavery, or from the "form of expression" for the Christian Doctrine of Slavery, for which I am contending, involves the same fallacy, with that which educes the doctrines of "passive obedience," and the "divine right of kings," from the Scripture deliverances on the subject of civil government.

The duty of obedience to "the powers that be," whether in the state or on the plantation, is a Christian duty, and is therefore enjoined in the word of God. The "doctrine of revolution," in the one case, and the "doctrine of emancipation," in the other, are not religious, but political doctrines, and therefore they are not taught us in the word of God. Of this, also, I shall have occasion to speak more fully in my next letter, and I therefore dismiss it for the present.

4. Nor does my statement imply that *a man may, without sin, hold slaves where the laws of the State prohibit it.*

The State is the proper authority to determine the question of the permission or prohibition of slavery within its own territory. And for a citizen to attempt to hold slaves, where the State prohibits slavery, is for him to "resist" the powers that be, in the sense of Rom. 13 : 2; and of such, Paul says, "They shall receive to themselves damnation."

Such are a few of the points, in which you have charged upon me opinions which I do not hold, and, upon my statement, consequences which I do not admit. And I make this distinct disclaimer, that if, in any future communication, you should see fit to renew these charges, it may rest upon you to show that their consequences are fairly involved in that statement.

Yours, truly,

GEO. D. ARMSTRONG.

DR. ARMSTRONG'S SECOND REJOINDER.

EMANCIPATION AND THE CHURCH.

To the Rev. C. Van Rensselaer, D.D.:

If I correctly apprehend the position you assume on the subject of "Emancipation and the Church," in your second letter, we agree in the main, whilst on secondary points only we differ.

SECTION I.—AGREEMENT AND DIFFERENCE.

What you assert for the Church is simply the right to utter opinions, or give advisory testimonies in favour of Emancipation; but not to make deliverances which shall bind the conscience, or in any way affect the standing of those who hold and act upon opinions different from those which she expresses. It was against the right of the Church to make the authoritative deliverances of the latter kind, that the argument of my second letter was mainly directed: and had I understood your position at first, as I do now, I should probably never have written that letter.

In so far, then, as authoritative deliverances are concerned, *we agree.*

The point on which *we differ,* is the right of the Church to utter opinions, or give advisory testimony in favour of emancipation.

You write—"Slavery has both moral and political aspects." "Our Church has always avoided interference with the State, in matters that are outside of her own appropriate work. She has not claimed authority over the political relations of slavery, nor attempted to extend her domain over subjects not plainly within her own province. It is only where slavery comes within the line of ecclesiastical jurisdiction; that is to say, in its moral and religious aspects, that our Church has maintained her right to deliver her testimony in such form, and at such times, as seemed best. She has 'rendered unto Cæsar the things that are Cæsar's, and unto God the things that are God's.' Let no one attempt to despoil her of this joy."

Here again, if I understand you, is a second point on which *we agree,* viz.: If the question of emancipation be properly a political question, the Church has no "right to deliver her testimony" respecting it, being estopped by God's law, which requires her to "render unto Cæsar the things that are Cæsar's."

We differ as to the category—religious or political—to which the question of emancipation belongs.

6

SECTION II.—IS THE QUESTION OF EMANCIPATION PROPERLY A POLITICAL QUESTION?

In my fourth letter, as well as in my "Christian Doctrine of Slavery," pp. 129, 130, I have endeavoured to draw the distinction between the "political" and "scriptural or Christian," in the doctrine of slavery; and if the positions there assumed are sound ones, then emancipation falls into the category of political questions, unless you can show either (1), That it is a question which "immediately concerns the interests of the life to come," and is not a question respecting "civil rights and political franchises;" or (2), That the word of God, when fairly interpreted, does contain a clear deliverance on the subject.

First. For proof that the Bible "treats the distinctions which slavery creates as matters of very little importance, in so far as the interests of the Christian life are concerned," and, consequently, the question of emancipation as not one which "immediately concerns the interests of the life to come," I refer you to "Christian Doctrine of Slavery," pp. 65–74.

In proof that the teaching of the Bible here corresponds with the experience of the Church, I refer you to the two incontrovertible facts—(1), That a larger proportion of the labouring classes belong to the Christian Church in the Southern States, where the labourers are mostly slaves, than in the Northern, where slavery does not exist; and (2), The number of coloured church members, in the evangelical churches in our Southern States, is nearly double that of all the evangelical churches gathered from among the heathen throughout the world. "In 1855 *heathen* church membership is set down at one hundred and eighty thousand. The present estimate of coloured church members in the Methodist Church South, is one hundred and seventy-five thousand. Eight or ten years ago the Baptist coloured membership at the South was recorded as only four thousand less than the Methodist. When to these two numbers, you add all the coloured members of other unincluded organizations of Methodists and Baptists, also of Episcopalians, Lutherans, and Presbyterians, you readily reach an aggregate of coloured church membership near twice as large as the strictly heathen orthodox church membership of the world." (Stiles's Modern Reform, p. 277.)

Second. Does the word of God, when fairly interpreted, contain a clear deliverance on this subject?

You find such a deliverance in 1 Cor. 7: 20, 21. "Let every man abide in the same calling wherein he was called. Art thou called being a servant? care not for it; but if thou mayest be made free, *use it rather*,"—and you write, "Use your freedom, rather," says Paul, expounding the nature of slavery, and throwing the light of inspiration upon its anomalous character. When did the Apostle ever exhort husbands and wives not to care for the marriage tie, and to seek to be freed from it, if the opportunity offered?

As I read this comment of yours, I could not but ask myself: Can my good brother Van Rensselaer have carefully studied this 7th chapter of 1 Cor.? Put the questions fairly, not—" when did the Apostle ever exhort husbands and wives not to care for the marriage tie, and to seek to be free from it if the opportunity offered," for the marriage tie, unlike that of slavery, cannot be dissolved by consent of parties; but " when did the Apostle ever exhort the unmarried not to care for the marriage tie, but being free from it, to retain their freedom." And I answer, in this very chapter. " I say therefore to the unmarried and widows, it is good for them that they abide even as I. Art thou loosed from a wife, seek not a wife. So then he that giveth her in marriage doeth well; but he that giveth her not in marriage doth better." Verses 8, 27, 38.

And this brings out my objection to the interpretation which you would put upon verse 21. Throughout the chapter, in answer to inquiries from the church at Corinth, Paul is giving instruction with especial regard to the circumstances in which they were placed at the time, and hence every special item of advice must be interpreted with this fact in view. Disregard this, in interpreting either the preceding portions of the chapter, or the parts which follow the passage under examination, and I see not how you can avoid the admission of doctrines clearly at variance with the teachings of other portions of the word of God; the Romish doctrine of the superior sanctity of a life of celibacy, for example.

Tried in either of these ways, then, emancipation falls into the category of political, and not that of religious questions. Nor will it avail to take it out of this category to show,—

1. *That the Church has often made deliverances on this subject in years that are passed.* From the close of the third until near the beginning of the present century a union of Church and State has existed throughout Christendom. In our country, for the first time since the days of Constantine, has the Church assumed that position of freedom which was her glory in apostolic days. It would be strange indeed if, in such circumstances, she has never transcended the limits which her great Head has prescribed; it would be more than could reasonably be expected, that she had yet fully comprehended her true position. Political preaching, and political church-deliverances, instead of being the novelty which some imagine them, date their origin as far back as the days when this union of Church and State was formed.

You quote the paper adopted by the Assembly in 1818 as containing such a deliverance respecting emancipation as you contend for; and you call my attention to the fact that my old instructor, Dr. George A. Baxter, " *clarum et venerabile nomen,*" was one of the committee of three by whom that paper was prepared. I know and admit all that you say about that paper. And I know also, that eighteen years afterwards, when Dr. Baxter was an older—and may I not add—a wiser man, he entertained and published very different views, as you will see by referring to his "Essay on the Abolition of Slavery," especially pp. 4 and 7. You quote, also, the paper adopted by the Synod of Virginia in 1800, and express the opinion that our Synod are ready to reaffirm this testimony in 1858. That you are mistaken here, you can easily satisfy yourself by reading the paper on slavery adopted in 1837, and the remarks made by the Virginia delegation in the convention which immediately preceded the separation of the Old from the New School, as reported in the second volume of Foote's Sketches of Virginia. You will there see that the ground assumed is precisely that which I occupy.

2. Nor will it avail to show *that emancipation has a bearing upon the well-being of a people—even their spiritual well-being.* Human advancement in every particular—the extension of commerce, the opening up of the country by railroads, improvements in agriculture and the mechanic arts—affects the spiritual well-being of man more or less directly. How could we, for instance, carry on the missionary operations of this nineteenth century but for the improvements of the nineteenth century? It is a mark of the heavenly origin of Christianity that she thus subsidizes every agency for God's service. And this, I believe, will be more and more the case as "the end" draweth nigh. But this by no means authorizes the Church to turn aside from her appropriate work, that she may supervise these agencies. In the days of her greatest glory, a prophet tells us that "there shall be upon the bells of the horses, holiness unto the Lord" (Zech. 14 : 20); but surely, he does not mean to teach us that in that day the Church of God will go into the business of bell-founding.

SECTION III.—MY POSITION.

Do not misapprehend the position I have assumed respecting this subject of Emancipation. It is not, that the word of God teaches that slavery is to be "a permanent institution, on a level with marriage and the parental relation," but that it treats the question of emancipation from slavery, just as it treats the analogous question of deliverance from despotic civil rule, as a political, and not a religious question, and hence, makes no deliverance on the subject. And further, that the Church is bound to treat them both alike, just as her Head has treated them in the instructions he has given her. And let me add, if you would convince the many "of like faith" with me on this point, you will have to show either (1.) That we place the question of emancipation in the wrong category; or (2.) That the Church has a right to meddle with politics.

SECTION IV.—A SECOND QUESTION.*

Thus far, I have discussed this subject of slavery, with the especial purpose of determining, if possible, the proper limits of ecclesiastical action. Let us look at it now from a different point of view, for the purpose of determining what our duty is, as citizens and Christian men, in a country where every citizen has a right to participation in the civil government.

To the general proposition, that all men are bound to seek the well-being, temporal and eternal, of their fellow-men, no one who receives the Bible as the word of God can possibly object. The injunctions, " Thou shalt love thy neighbour as thyself," and " All things whatsoever ye would that men should do to you, do ye even so to them," in their true scope and plain import, place this duty beyond all question.

How, then, can we best promote the well-being, temporal and eternal, of the slave race which in God's providence is among us ?

SECTION V.—POPULAR ERRORS.

Before attempting to answer this second question directly, let me turn your attention, briefly, to certain popular errors which, if I mistake not, lie at the foundation of the false reasoning current respecting the slave race in our country.

I. *It is a mistake to suppose that the slaves among us have any intelligent desire for freedom.*

Could you go from man to man among them, and ask of each the question—Do you desire to be free?—from very many, and these the best and most thoughtful of them, you would receive a decided answer in the negative; and I speak what I know when I say this. From others you would receive a different answer. But sit down, now, and question them, for the purpose of ascertaining what is the idea they attach to the word freedom, and in ninety-nine cases out of a hundred you will find that the only idea of freedom they have is the idea of exemption from labour. But is exemption from labour freedom ? Or, can any one confer such freedom as this upon man, until the work of human redemption is complete, and the Son of God has rolled back the curse laid upon " man sinning" in the sentence, " In the sweat of thy face shalt thou eat bread, till thou return unto the ground ; for out of it wast thou taken : for dust thou art and unto dust shalt thou return ?"

In confirmation of the above statement, let me call your atten-

---

* All this discussion about plans of emancipation appeared to the Editor *new* matter, foreign to the question of " Emancipation and the Church," and to the nature of a *rejoinder*. The Editor suggested to Dr. Armstrong the propriety of publishing it as a separate article, a sort of appendix to the series. But Dr. Armstrong having objected to this, courtesy to him required the publication of his letter, just as he wrote it. In the Reply to this second Rejoinder, the Editor will feel at liberty, either not to notice this new matter at all, or notice it now or hereafter, according to circumstances.—ED.

tion to the two facts, apparently contradictory, which it alone explains. (1.) That our slaves are the most contented, cheerful class of labourers on the face of the earth, and (2.) That the fugitive slaves in the Northern States and Canada are the most idle and worthless class in the communities to which they have gone.

II. *A second error respects the rights of the slave race in our country.*

1. Whatever may be affirmed respecting human rights in the abstract, practically, no man has a right to that which he is incapable of using with benefit to himself and safety to society. Or, applying this general principle to the case before us—in the words of Dr. Hodge, as quoted by you in your first Letter—"*the right to personal liberty is conditioned by the ability to exercise beneficially that right.*" If then the slave race among us do not possess the ability " to exercise beneficially the rights" of freemen—and I know that you will agree with me that such is the fact at the present time—it follows that their present slavery involves no violation of any right of theirs to freedom, for they have no such right. Do not say this reasoning involves the perpetuity of slavery. The right to personal freedom, and the right to such improvement as may ultimately fit them for freedom, are entirely different things ; and with perfect consistency, I deny the one, whilst I fully admit the other ; and before I close this letter, I will show you just how I think their claim under the last-mentioned right is to be met and satisfied.

2. " *The right to labour*"—in the true sense of that much-abused expression—that is, the right of every one willing and able to earn a living, to have that living, is a common right, belonging to every man, and a right which cannot be forfeited, excepting by such crime as forfeits life itself. So reason teaches ;—so teaches the word of God,—" And God said, Behold, I have given you"—i. e. Adam, our common parent—" every herb bearing seed, which is upon the face of all the earth, and every tree, in the which is the fruit of a tree yielding seed ; to you it shall be for meat" (Gen. 1 : 29, compare with 9 : 3). And every state of society which fails to secure this right, is vicious in so far as it fails. And every civil government which does not protect this right of the weak and poor, against the rich and powerful, is faulty in so far as it does not protect it. This right is one of the most precious temporal rights which the poor man has, for on this his comfort and his very life depend.

This right is secured under the system of slavery which exists in our country to a poor, degraded race of labourers, not only better than it could be secured to the same race under a system of free labour, but better than it is secured to a more elevated race of labourers in Europe, under any of the systems which prevail among the civilized nations of the Old World. In this most important particular, a system of slavery, instead of interfering with man's right, secures it.

III. *It is an error to attribute the suffering, and vice, and crime, apparent among our slaves, to their slavery.*

Official returns show that the suffering, and vice, and crime, apparent among the portion of the African race in slavery in our country, are far less than will be found among the portion of their race in freedom. As well might we attribute the suffering and crime among the manufacturing population in England—and if we may believe the sworn testimony taken before commissions of Parliament, the amount of suffering, at the least, is greater there than here—to manufactures; or the suffering and crime of the degraded portion of the white population in the Northern States to their freedom, as that among our slaves to their slavery.

The truth with respect to this matter is—as both observation and the word of God teach us—that suffering, and vice, and crime are the proper fruits of human degradation, and this degradation is a consequence of sin. Where, for a series of generations, a people have been sinking under the degrading influence of sin, no form of government, civil or social, can sever that connection which God has established between sin and degradation, on the one hand, and sin and suffering on the other. In the case of a degraded race situated as the African race in our country is, in so far as slavery exerts any influence, it is to diminish the amount of suffering, and vice, and crime among them, and not to increase it.

IV. *A fourth error is in attributing the degradation of our slaves to their slavery.*

That this degradation did not originate with slavery is placed beyond all question, by comparing our slaves with their countrymen in Africa, who have never left their native shores.

That it has not perpetuated this degradation, will be rendered equally evident by comparing the slaves among us now, with the same race when brought to this country. ·I doubt whether history furnishes us with an instance in which a deeply degraded race have made more rapid progress, upward and onward, than has been made by this race since their introduction among us.

The general reasoning we often hear on this subject is fallacious, if I mistake not, because it takes no account of the grand obstacle to the elevation of a degraded people; and that grand obstacle is idleness. If history teaches anything clearly, it is that you can never elevate a people in the scale of civilization, unless you can bring them to labour. From what I have seen of the African race in our country, I fully concur with Dr. Baxter in the opinion, "If the Southern slaves were emancipated in a body, and placed in a community by themselves, from their unwillingness to labour, they would sink into a savage state, and live by the chase, or the spontaneous productions of the earth, or else they would establish new forms of slavery among themselves." (Essay on Abolition of Slavery, p. 7.)

To a people such as the slave race in our country, the effect of slavery is elevating and not degrading. History points us to but one way—in so far as civil and political agencies are concerned—in which a deeply degraded race has ever yet been fitted for freedom; and that is, through the operation of a system of slavery, gradually ameliorating as the people were prepared for its amelioration. In this way our Anglo-Saxon race, once deemed by Cicero unfit even for slaves, but now in the van of civilization, worked their way up to freedom.

SECTION VI.—EMANCIPATION LAWS.

In approaching this subject of emancipation, there are certain points on which, I doubt not, we agree; and it may be well to note them distinctly at the outset. They are, (1.) Present emancipation would be a curse and not a blessing to our slaves; and (2.) Emancipation, with the prospect of the emancipated slaves remaining in this country, is neither practicable nor desirable, unless the slave race could be greatly elevated above their present position before obtaining their freedom.

The plan of emancipation which you would favour is substantially that adopted by the Northern States, near the beginning of the present century, with the addition of a provision for the removal to Africa of the emancipated slaves.

This plan embraces three particulars, viz. :

1. A law prospective in its operation—say that all slaves born after a certain year shall become free at the age of twenty-five.

2. Provision for the instruction of those to be emancipated in the rudiments of learning.

3. Provision for their transfer and comfortable settlement in Africa when they become free.

To all such plans as this I have several objections, for which I will ask a candid and careful examination.

Objection 1st. I believe that any such law would, in its practical working, prove, to a very large extent, *a transportation* and not an *emancipation* law.

Such was the fact with respect to the laws adopted in the New England and Northern States. In his "Modern Reform Examined" (p. 31), Dr. Stiles makes the statement: "When emancipation laws forbade the prolongation of slavery at the North, there are living witnesses who saw the crowds of negroes assembled along the shores of New England and the Middle States, to be shipped to latitudes where their bondage could be perpetuated; and their posterity toil to-day in the fields of the Southern planter." In confirmation of this statement of Dr. Stiles, I can show you in Virginia, some fifty of the descendants of these very transported slaves, proved to be such by the records of our courts: and I will add, it was the bringing out of this fact, in the course of a trial upon which I attended, about fifteen years ago, that first distinctly turned my attention to this matter.

When a few years ago it was proposed to make Missouri a free State by the operation of such a law, so strongly did this same tendency manifest itself, that the friends of a proper emancipation—Dr. N. L. Rice among the number—were obliged to lift their voice against it, declaring that it would be better to have no emancipation at all than such an one as this. In truth, the New England and Northern States, although they had but a small number of slaves at the time they became "free States," never did emancipate a large part of that number. Their so-called emancipation laws were, to a large extent, practically transportation laws; and the transportation of slaves by accumulating them on a smaller area, is detrimental, and not beneficial to the slaves themselves.

I call your attention to this fact, not to reproach the North—for it is not by crimination and recrimination the cause of truth is to be promoted—but to show you, in the light of history, what the practical working of these "prospective emancipation acts" is likely to be.

Objection 2d. But supposing the objection just stated could be obviated in some way—by the modern "compensation" scheme, for example—I object to the plan, on the ground that you cannot prepare the slave race among us for freedom by any short course of education, such as that proposed. Often, when a child, did I hear repeated the proverb, "there is no royal road to learning." And so may we say of a degraded race in slavery, "there is no royal road to freedom."

Let me give you the result of an experiment of my own on this point. Some eighteen years ago, I had living in my family a young slave woman, who seemed anxious to become free and to go to Liberia. She was a person of good character, and had been recently married to a man also of good character, who seemed like-minded with herself. After consulting with her husband's master, a personal friend of mine, and ascertaining that he was willing to adopt a similar course with him, I advanced the money for her purchase, with the understanding that she was to remain in my service until it was repaid. In the way proposed, the two became free when from 32 to 35 years of age. In the meantime, they were taught to read, and in other ways the effort was made to fit them for freedom. The result of all this has been that, instead of sending two good colonists to Liberia, my friend and I have added two to the number of free negroes in Virginia.

Were this a solitary case, I might think it an exceptional one. But after I began to get my eyes open to the probable result in this case, I was led to inquire into the result in other cases of like nature. And I can give you case upon case, with names and dates, where similar experiments have resulted in the same way.

But, perhaps, some may say they ought to have been compelled, for their own good, to go to Liberia. To all such suggestions as this, my reply is, (1.) It is vain to expect to make good citizens for Liberia by sending them there against their will, like convicts to a penal colony. (2.) We deceive ourselves when we speak of Africa as "their native country," "their home." Africa is no more a "native country," "a home," to our slaves, in their own apprehension, than the North of Ireland is my country, or Holland is yours. (3.) Emancipation laws which compel expatriation are cruel in their practical operation, since they involve the sundering of ties both of kindred and affection,—and thus revive, under another name, one of the harshest features of slavery, a feature which has now, practically, almost disappeared from the slavery existing in our country.

Objection 3d. I have yet a third objection to the plan of emancipation we are considering, and it is that I see not the least prospect of Liberia being able to do the part assigned it in this plan for a long time to come—certainly not while you and I, my good brother, have a part in what is done under the sun—if the work of colonization is to be carried on with due regard to the safety of the colony, or a proper attention to the wants and claims upon us of the African race in our country.

In order that you may understand my objection, let me set before you certain thoughts and opinions on the subject of Liberia Colonization, and let me ask for them a candid consideration.

SECTION VII.—CAPACITY OF LIBERIA FOR IMMIGRATION.

In all our calculations about Liberia, we must remember that she is yet an infant colony, and that the greatest danger which does now or has yet threatened her, is from the too rapid immigration of such colonists as we are able to send her.

On this point, Rev. J. Leighton Wilson—eighteen years a missionary in Africa—writes: "The directors of the colonization enterprise, we think, have erred in directing their efforts too exclusively to the one object of transporting emigrants to Liberia. Many regard the number actually sent out as the true, if not the only test of the prosperity of the enterprise. But this is a serious mistake, *and if adhered to much longer may prove the ruin of the cause.* It requires something more than mere numbers to constitute a thrifty and flourishing commonwealth. On the other hand, an undue accumulation of idleness, improvidence, and vice, such as would be likely to accrue from thrusting large numbers of these people indiscriminately into the bosom of this infant republic, would certainly result in its entire overthrow." (Western Africa, p. 410.)

Rev. D. A. Wilson—principal of the Alexander High School in Liberia—in the October Number of the Presbyterian Magazine, writes: "A mere passage across the Atlantic works no transformation of character. Would that Colonizationists would think of this, and regulate their actions accordingly. Would that masters in emancipating their slaves would remember it, and learn that their first duty is, not to emancipate them, but to prepare them for freedom. *Indiscriminate immigration has been a great curse to Liberia."*

That we may form some idea—upon reliable data—of what a republic can do in the way of assimilating an immigrant population, let us call to mind the experience of our own country. We number not far from thirty million of the best portion of the human race. Our average immigration is not far from a quarter of a million annually; and these immigrants are certainly as far advanced in all that fits them for becoming good citizens as any we can hope to send to Africa for a long time to come. And yet, this nation is tasked to the utmost to assimilate this immigration, and no thoughtful patriot would be willing to see it greatly increased at the present time.

SECTION VIII.—TRUE FIELD OF OPERATION FOR COLONIZATION.

The Colonization Society was formed, and the colony of Liberia founded, not to operate as an adjunct to a general emancipation, but with a very different object.

The second article of the constitution of the American Colonization Society declares, " The object to which its attention is to be *exclusively* directed, is to promote and execute a plan for colonizing, with their own consent, the *free people of colour* residing in our country, in Africa, or such other place as Congress shall deem expedient."

In order to a fair understanding of the case, let me ask your attention to the following points.

I. The African race in America consists of two distinct classes, viz. : the free people of colour, and slaves. The number of the first-mentioned class is now not far from half a million, of whom rather more than one-half are resident in the slave States ; the remainder in the free States.

II. In so far as any claim upon us is concerned—either on the ground of our common humanity, or any wrong done to their fathers by our fathers in their original transfer to this country—the two classes stand upon precisely the same footing. Neither class can claim precedence of the other.

III. The present condition of the free people of colour, in this country, is worse than that of our slaves; and their condition in the free States is worse than in the slave States. For proof of this I refer you to the statistics of " pauperism" and " crime" in the census returns for 1850.

IV. The portion of the race in slavery are rapidly multiplying, and gradually rising in all that constitutes civilization, in the best sense of that word; whilst the portion of the race in freedom in the free States, like the poor Indians, are fading; and must ere long perish, unless something more can be done for them than has yet been done.

V. The portion of the race in freedom furnishes the best and most hopeful subjects for Liberian colonization. The representations given by some—not pro-slavery men—of this class as "a debased and degraded set"—"more addicted to crime, and vice, and dissolute manners than any portion of the people"—"a pestiferous class, whose increase in Ohio would be the increase of crime, misery, and want, to a fearful extent," whilst true of them as a class, as the census returns proved beyond all question, yet fails to make a distinction which truth requires at our hands. Among this degraded class there is to be found a number, say one in ten, of the most intelligent and best prepared for successful colonization, of all the African race in our country. "Many of them have been emancipated either for merit in themselves or their ancestors" (Governor Wise); and the deteriorating effects of freedom, in contact with the white man, must have been rapid, indeed, if this be not the case.

To these, my observation would teach me, that we ought to add, say one more in every ten, who are as well prepared for colonization as those who would be sent to Africa under the operation of such schemes of emancipation as that we are considering.

Thus it appears that one-fifth, or one hundred thousand of the free coloured people of our country, are as well or better prepared for colonization, on the coast of Africa, than the portion of the African race now in slavery.

Bring together, now, these facts. These two classes, the free coloured people and the slaves, have an equal claim upon us, in so far as our common humanity or wrong done to their fathers is concerned. The present condition of the one is worse than that of the other. The one, unless it can be saved by colonization, or some other such instrumentality, must ere long perish, whilst the other is multiplying and improving; and this portion, more miserable at the present time and in prospect, yet will furnish a large body of colonists, better fitted for successful colonization than those which will be procured from the other portion. And does not every principle of a wise, Christian philanthropy require us to adhere to the course marked out by the founders of the Colonization Society, and attend first to the free people of colour, and only after our work here has been done, to think of resorting to colonization as an adjunct to emancipation?

SECTION IX.—WHAT THE COLONIZATION SOCIETY HAS DONE.

At the close of my second letter, in a quotation from Bishop Hopkins, a small portion of those now in slavery are pointed out as proper subjects for colonization in Africa. These would become free in the natural course of things, and in all such calculations ought to be counted with free persons of colour.

It is from this class, I believe, most of the colonists, hitherto sent to Liberia, have been obtained. Of the five hundred and eighty-seven persons carried by the Mary C. Stevens, sixty-three only were born free. (See Forty-first Annual Report of Colonization Society, pp. 13, 14.) As yet, then, the Colonization Society has hardly touched the large class of free coloured persons in our country.

The Colonization Society was formed in 1817, but not until 1824 can the colony of Liberia be considered as fairly established. Since then thirty-four years have elapsed, and the colony now numbers about ten thousand, of whom but a part, say three thousand, are from the class of free coloured persons in our country.

SECTION X.—WHAT LIBERIAN COLONIZATION MAY REASONABLY BE EXPECTED TO DO.

1. I have already directed your attention to the grand obstacle to rapid immigration, in so far as Liberia is concerned, viz.: the difficulty in assimilating such an immigration as we are able to send her.

On the subject of "Christian appliances," as you term them, in their relation to the rate of immigration, listen to Rev. J. Leighton Wilson: "Another thing against which it behooves these missionary societies to be guarded, is that of doing too much for the Liberians, in the way of providing gratuitous education and preaching. We regard it as one of the chief failings of the Liberians, and one of the most serious hindrances to their improvement, that they are too willing to be taken care of. They have no self-supporting schools; very little has been done to support the Gospel among themselves; and there is a disposition to look to the missionary societies to do everything of the kind for them, and the sooner they are *taught* to depend upon themselves the better." (Western Africa, p. 410.)

2. The grand obstacle to a rapid emigration, on the part of the free people of colour in our country, is their deep-rooted distrust of the capacity of their own people for safely conducting the affairs of government. This obstacle is well set forth in the language of a young free coloured man I had in my employ for four years, endeavouring to fit and persuade him to go to Liberia, when be put an end to the matter by saying, "I know more of negroes than you do, and I had rather live among white folks."

Both of these obstacles are of such a nature as to require time to overcome them, and to teach us the absolute necessity of great prudence in the management of African colonization.

If now it has taken us thirty-four years to place a colony of ten thousand, about three thousand of whom are from the class of "free persons of colour," on the coast of Africa, when can we reasonably calculate that our work will be done with the one hundred thousand who remain, and who, upon every ground of sound policy as well as humanity, claim precedence of the portion of their race in slavery?

"Across that bridge of boats," said a certain eloquent speaker, referring to the line of steamships which it was proposed that the General Government should establish between this country and Liberia, "there will go, with a tramp like an army with banners, a mighty crowd, whose exodus will be more glorious than the exodus of Israel." Well, it would be an easy matter for our people to build this "bridge of boats." It would be, comparatively, an easy matter to start the "mighty crowd," amid the waving of banners and great rejoicing; but what is to become of them at the other end of the bridge? I confess, there is no vision rises before my eyes but that which Dr. Baxter saw, the vision of this "mighty crowd," through "unwillingness to labour, sinking into the savage state, and living by the chase, or the spontaneous productions of the earth, or else establishing new forms of slavery among themselves."

And can I, as a God-fearing man, favour any scheme involving such a catastrophe as this? I may be mistaken in my opinions respecting this matter, but they are opinions honestly entertained, and not hastily adopted. I am a friend to Liberian colonization. I have confidence in its accomplishment of great good if prudently conducted; and it is because I am a friend, that I deprecate any such measures as are contemplated in the popular emancipation schemes.

SECTION XI.—THE WORK AND THE WAY.

Is there nothing we can do, and do now, for the slave race among us?

I reply, yes; there is much that can be done; work at which we may labour now, work for the Church, work for the Christian citizen, work for the philanthropist, and all of it work which will tell upon the slave race, and their preparation for ultimate freedom, if freedom be what God in his providence has in store for them.

As I read the lesson which history teaches—and in revelation I find no deliverance on the subject—there is but one way in which a people, in whose case the process of degradation by sin has been going on through many generations, and upon whom, in consequence thereof, slavery has come, can be raised and fitted for freedom again, and that one way is through the agency of a gradually ameliorating slavery, the amelioration taking place as they are prepared to profit by it. *Individual* exceptions will occur, as stated at the close of my second letter, but for a *race*, history points to no other way. In this way our Anglo-Saxon race, once sunk under a more galling slavery than the African has ever suffered in our country, was prepared for freedom.

This process of amelioration is going on, and has been going on ever since the introduction of new bodies of slaves, through the agency of the slave-trade, ceased. Many of the cruel laws, once necessary to restrain a barbarous people, have disappeared from our statute-books, whilst the others have become, to a very large extent, a dead letter, and, in the natural order of things, will disappear.

For all such amelioration, Christianity lays the only sure foundation. The Church of God, without departing from the letter of her instructions, without stepping aside at all from the course which Christ has marked out for her, must do a great work in preparing the way for any amelioration of slavery, safe and profitable for the slaves themselves; and when the Church has once done her work, the Christian citizen and the philanthropist will do what remains to be done.

But for unreasonably protracting this letter, I would present this matter more in detail. As it is, I must refer you for a fuller exhibition of the scheme to the " Christian Doctrine of Slavery," pp. 117–136.

SECTION XII.—EFFECTS OF ENTERTAINING THIS EMANCIPATION SCHEME.

As I have remarked, I have no confidence in the happy operation of any general emancipation scheme; at least, for a long time to come; and the present agitation of the matter is doing harm, and has been doing harm for some years past, both North and South. As Dr. Hodge has well said, " The great duty of the South is not emancipation, but improvement;" and, if I mistake not, the present agitation of emancipation has been the principal means of turning aside attention from the present duty.

At the South, it has, in so far as it has operated at all, diverted attention from our present duty,—the religious instruction and gradual elevation of the African race among us. Never, until we look the matter fully in the face, and come to understand that there is no short process by which we can be rid of our responsibility, will we be prepared to do all our duty in this behalf.

At the North, it has turned aside the attention of Christian men from their own appropriate field of labour. You have some two hundred thousand of this African race in the free States, and their present condition is worse than that of the portion of the race at the South, as the census statistics of " pauperism and crime" abundantly prove; and their future prospects are no better than their present condition.

What are you doing for them? Ameliorating your laws? Not that I hear of. Colonizing them in Africa? Once in a great while I hear of a small band leaving the Northern States for Liberia ; but the great mass of colonists are from the Southern States.

D 3

Are you trying to educate them for better things? Here I rejoice that I can answer—at least for our Church—in a different tone. You have founded the Ashmun Institute. And that God's rich blessing may rest upon it, should be the prayer of every intelligent friend of Africa. But besides this, I hear of nothing that Christian men at the North are doing in this way. And what is more, whilst at the South it is often a subject of anxious inquiry, in our Church councils and in the private circle, what can we do for this people who, in God's providence, are made dependent on us?—I hear of no such inquiry at the North. Indeed, the only action I have heard of, for some years past, even by any of our conservative synods, is that of which you tell me in your second letter,—the re-affirming of "the testimony of 1818" by the Synod of Pittsburg and Ohio, which, to take the best view of it, is a telling one's neighbours what they ought to do, instead of asking what can I do in the field which God's providence has assigned to me?

It is in no spirit of retaliation that I write this; but that I may show you what the effect of a premature agitation of the Emancipation question has been. And could I reach my conservative brethren at the North, and "speak a word in their ear," I would say, Take care, lest you find occasion for the lamentation, "They made me keeper of the vineyards, but mine own vineyard have I not kept."

SECTION XIII.—REMARKS ON DR. VAN RENSSELAER'S THIRD LETTER.

1. Most of your third letter is based upon a misapprehension, for which I frankly acknowledge that I am to blame. When I wrote—"The correctness of this brief history of *anti-slavery* opinions," &c.—I thoughtlessly used the word *anti-slavery* in a literal sense, but not the sense which it has in the current use of the day. By reading the extract from Bishop Hopkins's "American Citizen," to which the sentence refers, you will see that I spoke of the opinion, "that the institution, in itself, involved a violation of religion and morality," the opinion which has given rise to "the assaults against the lawfulness of the institution." This is the peculiar type of anti-slavery opinion distinguished as abolitionism; and *abolition opinion* is the expression I ought to have used.

In addition to the proof already given of the correctness of the statement of Bishop Hopkins, in the paragraph referred to, viz., "If we go on from the days of the Apostles to examine the doctrine and practice of the Christian Church, we find no other views entertained on the subject"—i. e., no other views than that "the institution, in itself, did not involve a violation of religion or morality," let me call your attention to one fact. "Most of the Fathers" (Hodge), "The Fathers of the Church from the time of

Chrysostom" (Olshausen), interpreted the passage chiefly relied upon by you, viz., 1 Cor. 7 : 21, to mean : " Art thou called being a slave, care not for it ; but even if thou canst be free, prefer to remain as thou art." (See Hodge on 1 Cor., Olshausen's Commentary.) I do not cite this as a correct interpretation of the passage, for I do not so receive it. I cite it simply to show you what the current sentiment of the ancient Church must have been when such an interpretation of this passage was commonly received.

2. In your letter, in two instances, you strangely confound things that differ. (1.) To declare that certain opinions respecting human liberty have originated in an infidel theory of civil government, is one thing. To declare that those who hold such opinions are infidels, is a very different thing. (2.) You confound opposition to slaveholding, with opposition to the African slave-trade, including in itself, as the latter always has and always will, man-stealing ; as if the lawfulness of the one implied the lawfulness of the other. Surely, the distinction made, in the law of Moses, in the New Testament, and in the laws of our own country, between slaveholding and man-stealing, i. e., "kidnapping free persons to be sold as slaves," is a sound distinction, and one that has a good foundation in the nature of the two things.

SECTION XIV.—CONCLUDING REMARKS.

1. In discussing, as I have, this "Second Question" (§ 4), I have been discussing a question which lies outside the proper range of the Church's action ; and I have done it, in part, to show you that such a limitation of the power of the Church, as I have contended for, does not imply the denial of any claim which the African race has upon us, either as men or as Christians. The key to my position is this : I see no good reason to believe that the African race in slavery among us will attain to that elevation requisite for a safe and profitable freedom, in any other way than that in which other races, once similarly situated, have risen. And if I cannot see distinctly a freedom for them in the future, it is for just the same reasons that I cannot see distinctly the future overthrow of despotic government throughout the earth. I know not how far this elevating process shall have proceeded ere this present dispensation shall close. "When shall the Son of Man come?" and "When the Son of Man cometh, shall he find faith on the earth?" And if I deprecate the raising of the question of emancipation now, it is on the same ground upon which I would adopt a similar course, were I a citizen of France, with respect to civil liberty, viz., it will do much present harm, and can do no possible present good.

2. In my statement of the "Christian doctrine of slavery," and in insisting upon the political character of the question of emancipation, I am contending for no mere abstraction. My doctrine, in

its practical operation, will forever exclude the "slavery question" from our Church councils—where its introduction has done nothing but harm—and will exclude it in precisely the way in which Christ and his apostles excluded it in their day, and yet leave the Church all the work which Christ has assigned her; and a glorious work it is,—a work which, well done, will confer upon the African race in our country benefits infinitely transcending all which the most perfect civil liberty on earth could confer.

When first my attention was particularly directed to the language used in 1 Tim. 6 : 1–5 (the passage quoted in my first Letter), that language seemed to me unaccountably harsh, directed, as it is, against what I thought a very innocent form of error. But as years have rolled on, and the character of the error there condemned has developed itself before my eyes, I have come to understand better why the Holy Ghost uses the language he does.

Trace the history of Abolitionism for the last twenty-five years, and mark its doings. What that is "true, or honest, or pure, or lovely, or of good report," in State or Church, which it has touched and not defiled,—or gotten into its power and not destroyed ?

It has made enemies of those once friends. It has broken up the communion of God's people. It has led even gray-haired ministers of the Gospel to revile their brethren of the same Church as "slave-driving hierarchs," for daring to stand up for God's truth as it was "delivered to the saints."

It has entered the pulpit, and banishing the Gospel of Christ, has substituted for it the preaching of narrow-minded, bitter, sectional politics. It has entered our catholic associations for purposes of Christian benevolence, and now, the "*American*" in the title of our "American Home Missionary Society," stands there, like the sculptured skull and cross-bones on some old tombstone, a memento of worth and piety departed. It has entered our church councils—and along with it have come strife and dissension. First, "railings, evil surmisings, and perverse disputings," have taken the place of Christian conference. And then, the ploughshare of division has been driven through "the heritage of God."

"O my soul, come not thou into their secret; unto their assembly, mine honour, be not thou united."

Yours, truly,
Geo. D. Armstrong.

DR. VAN RENSSELAER'S FIRST REJOINDER.

ON THE PROPER STATEMENT OF THE SCRIPTURAL DOCTRINE OF SLAVERY.

To THE REV. GEORGE D. ARMSTRONG, D.D.

An amicable discussion of slavery, instead of suggesting to you "the dark and bloody ground" of Kentucky, with its scenes of savage warfare, only required our presence on the field of scriptural truth. The appearance of brother Armstrong, with rifle in hand, is not a pleasant clerical sight, introduced by the law of association into the perspective; nor is it a very terrible one, for I have discovered that, even with the aim of so good a marksman as himself, a rifle-shot is "not necessarily and in all circumstances" exact.

Your allusion to "the shrieks for freedom" is the first political allusion made in our discussion, and this footprint upon the "dark and bloody ground," leading into a trail of the wilderness, I respectfully decline to follow.

Your remark that sections and divisions "secure perspicuity" and "guard against misapprehension," is a very good one.

SECTION I.—DR. ARMSTRONG ADMITS THE TRUTH OF MY GENERAL PROPOSITION.

The issue between us is whether my proposition that "slaveholding is not necessarily and in all circumstances sinful," is liable to just exception as an inexact, or inadequate, expression of the scriptural doctrine in the premises; or whether your proposition that "slaveholding is not a sin in the sight of God" is more accurate and complete. The characteristic difference in the phraseology of the two propositions is that mine has a special reference to *circumstances*, whilst you deny the right to admit them. Your own incidental concessions decide that the introduction of circumstances is right and necessary.

§ 1. You expressly declare, among the articles of your faith on this subject, that "slavery is expedient or inexpedient, right or wrong, *according to circumstances.*" p. 68. I have substituted, as you permit, "slavery" for "civil despotism;" and here I find my own proposition written down as true by Dr. Armstrong, under "circumstances" quite remarkable in an objector. I am aware that you maintain that this doctrine is not deducible entirely from

Scripture, but that it is partly deducible from reason, and includes a political view. This point I shall examine presently. All that I desire you to notice now, is that my proposition, irrespective of the mode of its proof, is really the *true one*, by your own admission.

§ 2. In your original Letter, you deny that "all slaveholding is sinless in the sight of God." Of course, some slaveholding is sinful; and what but circumstances must determine its character? You also explicitly declare that, "when we state the proposition, that slaveholding is not a sin in the sight of God, it can apply to such slaveholding only as subsists in conformity with the law of God." p. 11 and 12. Here again, do not circumstances decide whether it is justifiable or not?

§ 3. You, over and over, admit, in your last Letter, that slavery classes with *adiaphora*, or things indifferent. Civil despotism, or slavery, "belongs in morals to the *adiaphora*, or things indifferent:" p. 68, 69, 72. Now the characteristic, formal nature of such things is that they are not *per se*, or necessarily and in all circumstances, either right or wrong, but that they may be either right or wrong *according to circumstances*.

With all these admissions in favour of my form of statement, made so clearly and palpably by yourself, it would be difficult to see what opening you leave for further assaults upon it, were it not for a distinction you set up between the *scriptural* and the *whole* view of the subject, which I shall proceed to examine. It is a great point gained, when Dr. Armstrong plainly concedes that the *whole*, or complete view of the subject demands the introduction of "circumstances," which is the chief point in dispute between us.

SECTION II.—DR. ARMSTRONG ON POLITICS; DISTINCTION
BETWEEN SCRIPTURE AND REASON, ETC.

The distinction you make between the scriptural and the political relations of the subject is one of the two significant points of your Rejoinder.

§ 1. Whilst my proposition is admitted to be right, in view of the *combined* testimony of Scripture and reason, you maintain that Scripture alone does not authorize it. Is not this, in effect, saying that the Bible is not a sufficient rule of faith and practice on the subject of slavery? Mark; we are not now discussing any of the questions of capital and labour, or any State plans of general emancipation. The question before us is one concerning our relations to God. It is the case, we will suppose, of a slaveholding member of your own church, whose conscience is agitated by the question of duty in regard to his slaves. Has he any other guidance for the general principles of his conduct, than his Bible? Can he go to the laws of the State for peace of mind? Or can his reason supply any light which has not its source in revelation? Do you say that this is not a question of morals ? I reply that you yourself admit that slavery " belongs in *morals* to the *adiaphora*." If so, it must be brought to the test of God's word, as interpreted by the best use of reason. On such a question as this, we cannot say, " this part of the doctrine comes from revelation, and that part from reason," or " slavery is right according to Scripture, but right or wrong according to politics." What we are aiming at is a general formula, embracing the moral principles by which slavery can be judged. And human reason, making its deductions from the general spirit, principles, and precepts of Scripture, deduces the *whole* doctrine, which has the authority of " Thus saith the Lord." According to your view, reason is an independent source of authority, going beyond the word of God, on this practical moral question ; whilst I maintain that reason finds in the Word of God the moral elements for the determination of duty, and must gather up the results of scriptural declarations with all care, and with subjection to the Divine authority. The great error of the abolitionists consists in running wild with your doctrine, and they undertake to declare by " reason" even what the Scriptures *ought* to teach.

§ 2. Your own declarations in regard to despotism and slavery, which we both place in the same category, show that the Scriptures actually cover the entire subject. You state, on p. 69, and also 80, that "the doctrines of passive obedience," and of "the Divine right of kings," are not implied in the scriptural injunctions to obey the powers that be, and to submit to every ordinance of man for the Lord's sake. That is to say, you admit that passive obedience is not a scriptural doctrine, or, in other words, that civil revolution is authorized, under certain circumstances, by the word of God. This is the doctrine our fathers taught and preached in the Revolutionary War, and which the Jacobites and non-juring divines in England resisted. This is true doctrine. And yet, on the same page, a few lines farther on, you inconsistently state that " the right of revolution is a political right, the doctrine of revolution a political doctrine ; and, *therefore,* we have no reason to expect that they will be taught us in the word of God ; I receive them as true *upon the authority of reason:*" p. 69. So that the conclusion you seem finally to reach is that " passive obedience" is the doctrine of Scripture ; but the right of revolution, the doctrine of reason ! And let it be noted, you come to this conclusion, although you had a few lines before, declared that passive obedience is "not implied" in the command to obey Nero ! The truth must lie somewhere in the confusion of these contradictory propositions ; and, in my judgment, it lies just here : resistance to tyrants may be justified by the Word of God ; and, therefore, the doctrine of revolution is a *scriptural* doctrine.

§ 3. Your attempted distinction between what is scriptural and what is political, is an entire fallacy, so far as the general principles of duty are concerned. You say that " the Scriptures were given to teach us religion and not politics;" p. 69. But is not "politics" the science of our duties and obligations to the State? The Bible regulates our duties to God, to ourselves, to our fellow creatures, and to the State. We owe no duty to the State that cannot be derived from the Bible. All our political duties are moral duties. Is not obedience a political duty? And does not the Bible place obedience on moral grounds—"wherefore, ye must needs be subject, not only for wrath, but also for conscience sake :" Rom. 13 : 5. All our duties to the State are taught in the Scriptures. The Word of God gives us the general principles of morality that apply to civil despotism and slavery, whilst the details about revolution and the plans of emancipation are political measures, which belong to the State. Your error is in saying that, emancipation being political, places it beyond the reach of the Bible and of the Church.

§ 4. I have, by no means, intended to deny that there is a broad distinction between the Church and the State, as likewise between each of these and the family. But this does not withdraw either, or all of them, from the reach of moral, religious, and Christian obligation. A wrong, immoral, or sinful act does not cease to be such, because it is done in the family or by the State. It is just as "properly sinful" as if done by an individual. If a community, in their political capacity license gambling, or prostitution, the act of granting the license, or using it, is none the less sinful in both parties, because it is done politically. If the people in any of these United States vote to establish a despotism with power to persecute Christianity, they do a wicked act. If the constitution and laws of Virginia should be so altered as to prohibit masters from teaching their slaves to read the Bible, all parties to such a proceeding would be guilty of sin. The State is under moral obligations to act righteously. Slaveholding, as it now exists in the southern portion of our country, may not now be, nor do I believe it is, a sinful relation on the part of the great body of the masters, nor does it involve sin on the part of the lawgivers simply for authorizing its present existence. But a condition of things may arise, in which what is now sinless may become sinful, whether allowed or not by the State. Things in their own nature sinful, or things indifferent in themselves which in given circumstances are inconsistent with Christian love, justice, and mercy, are not made otherwise, because authorized by the civil power. The continuance of slavery by law, when "well being" and "the general good" require emancipation, would be sinful.

§ 5. A singular climax is reached by your statement, that, when you say, civil despotism, or slavery, is "expedient or inexpedient, right or wrong, according to circumstances," you "do not mean wrong *in the proper sense of sinful*:" p. 69. Then, my dear Doctor, why use the word at all? In what sense do you use it? If wrong does not properly mean "sinful," what does "right" properly mean? and what does "morals" properly mean? and what does *adiaphora* properly mean? Is any meaning better determined than the ordinary meaning of "right and wrong?" Do these terms, in moral questions, ever fail to denote the moral quality of actions and relations? Ought right and wrong to have two meanings in a minister's vocabulary?

It is, indeed, not to be denied that some things, in themselves indifferent, may be inexpedient, which could not at the same time be pronounced sinful. Such things as protective tariffs and free trade, greater or less costliness of dress or equipage, in certain circumstances, might be put into this category. But there are others again, whose inexpediency arises from the *circumstances* that render them *immoral*, or direct instruments of immorality and irreligion. They are inexpedient, because, though in some circumstances innocent, yet in the circumstances in question, they are immoral. The mere sale, or use, of ardent spirits is a thing indifferent. It is sinful or sinless, according to circumstances. But, if a man were to keep a tippling shop, in which he derives his profits from pandering to vicious appetites and making drunkards of the young men of a community, this is criminal and unchristian, although he could show a thousand licenses from the civil authority for doing it. The same would be true of engaging in the African slave trade, although Southern convention after convention were to favour it, and the Federal Government were to sanction it. And, in general, to take your own expression, any slaveholding, which does not "subsist in conformity to the law of God," is of the same character. Although there are *adiaphora* in the sphere of religion and politics which may be deemed inexpedient without being pronounced sinful, there are others which are inexpedient, because, in the circumstances, the doing of them inevitably involves sin. Of this sort, is the *procuring*, or *the holding* of slaves, in *circumstances* which make it contrary to Christian love, justice, and mercy. And it alters not the moral nature of such conduct to label it " political."

§ 6. It is deserving of notice that slaveholding is not a political institution in the sense that it is made obligatory by law. A slaveholder can emancipate his slaves in Virginia at any time he sees proper, or his conscience will allow; and notwithstanding certain restrictions in some of the States, it is believed that in none is the subject altogether withdrawn from the master's control. In your State, the continuance or discontinuance of slaveholding is a question, depending, indeed, upon considerations of the social and public welfare, but yet not requiring political action. Emancipation has been generally regarded, in such cases, as a benevolent, moral, or religious act, and it is performed by the individual in the fear of God, without reference to the powers that be. The general spirit of the laws, as well as of public opinion, may be even opposed to emancipation; and yet the individual, as a citizen, has a perfect right to give freedom to his slaves. In such cases, in what sense is the continuance or discontinuance of slaveholding "in part a *political* doctrine, which it is the business of the statesman to expound, and the civil ruler to apply?" Granting, however, certain political relations, I have shown that this does not exclude the general principles of the Bible from controlling the subject.

§ 7. Nor does it alter anything, so far as our present issue is concerned, to say that what the Scriptures teach is one thing, and what I know by the natural faculties is another thing. The distinction between these things is important, and where the teachings of reason and revelation are in conflict, requires us to submit reason to revelation. But it does not admit of the possibility of two contradictory beliefs in the same mind, at the same time, in regard to the same subject. I cannot believe on the authority of Scripture that all slaveholding is sinless, and on the authority of my reason that some slaveholding is sinful. These propositions exclude each other. If I believe one to be true on whatever evidence, I cannot, at the same time, believe the other to be true, on any evidence whatsoever. Now, as Dr. Armstrong admits, with Dr. Hodge, p. 72, that, in some circumstances, domestic slavery may be wrong and unjust, and that it is so in circumstances involving a violation of the Divine law, p. 6, you must hold what you call your scriptural doctrine that "slaveholding is not a sin in the sight of God" in the sense of a particular and not a universal proposition, *i. e.*, that *some* slaveholding is not a sin—and not that *all* slaveholding is sinless, and consequently you must hold that the former of these two last statements, gives the true and exact Scripture doctrine, and the *whole* doctrine, too.

Withal, your proposition, that "slaveholding is not a sin in the sight of God" is not in the language of Scripture. And, even if it were, it is only necessary to remember that a proposition, which is a general one in its form, is often in reality, like yours, a particular one. It is one of the simplest laws of interpretation, that, where the extent in which the subject of a proposition is used, is not determined by such qualifying adjuncts as "some," "all," "every," &c., we must infer it from other things which show the writer's meaning. Those who are conversant with Arminian and Universalist polemics, know how often it is necessary to adopt some exegetical qualification. When your meaning is explicated in full and exact expression, it emerges into precisely my own proposition. Your distinction between Scripture and reason is, *quoad hoc*, utterly pointless. Nor does it require a very high exercise of the "natural faculties" to see this.

§ 8. It is with some surprise that I find you saying that you accept some things as true, but not as binding upon the conscience. You say, "the first statement [yours] sets forth truth which must bind the conscience, and exactly defines the limits of Church power. The latter [mine] though I *receive it as true*, does *neither the one* nor the other:" p. 70. The fact is, to a conscientious man this is a sheer impossibility. So far as a man believes a given proposition to be true, he is bound, and feels bound in conscience, to act as if it were true. Some propositions and truths are, indeed, more immediately ethical in their nature than others, and thus speak more directly to the conscience. Among the first, and self-evident principles of ethics is this, that we ought to cleave and conform to the truth. The proposition that two and two make four is not a scriptural or ethical proposition. Neither is the proposition that our country is increasing in population with unexampled rapidity. But he, who regards them as true, is bound by Scripture and conscience to act as if they were so. He sins in doing otherwise. The Bible does not explicitly announce every true thing which we are to believe, and to be bound by in our conduct, although its principles lead to it. It assumes that a multitude of things, which control our interpretation and application of it, are known otherwise. And it enjoins us, "if there be any virtue," to regard "whatsoever things are true, whatsoever things are honest, whatsoever things are just, whatsoever things are pure, whatsoever things are lovely, whatsoever things are of good report:" Phil. 4 : 8. Whatever, therefore, you believe to be true respecting slaveholding, must bind your conscience. Slaveholding can never get beyond the authority of conscience and the Bible.

SECTION III.—DR. ARMSTRONG ON THE GENERAL ASSEMBLY.

In showing that my form of statement was coincident with that of the General Assembly, a comparison was instituted between it and all the deliverances of the Assembly from 1787 to 1845. You carefully avoid any reference to any action of the General Assembly, except the one of 1845, which is the only one you venture to claim as in any respect covering your ground. Why is this, Doctor? Are you afraid of the whole light? Or do you think that the action of 1845 was scriptural, whilst all the previous action was only deducible by "reason?" Or do you believe that the testimony of 1845 was contrary to, and subversive of, the testimony of 1787 and of 1818? If you take the latter ground, then I beg you to remember that the Assembly of 1846 passed the following resolution: "Resolved, That in the judgment of this House, the action of the General Assembly of 1845 was not intended to deny or rescind the testimony often uttered by the General Assemblies previous to that date," Baird's Digest, 814. So you perceive that the Assembly's testimony is one harmonious whole.

But without pressing you further on this point, I turn to your singular evasions of the forms of statements adopted by the Assembly of 1845. These forms are obviously, both in spirit and in words, so precisely like my own, that the only method of getting round them is to raise the cry of "abolition!" Your argument is that, because the abolitionists use a certain form of expression, therefore, the expressions of the Assembly, which are similar but in the *negative*, are "like poor land, which the more a man has, the worse off he is." Now does not my good Brother Armstrong know that it makes no difference from what quarter the language comes, provided the Assembly judged it suitable to give expression to its own opinions? But such a trivial objection—which is worth to a controversialist about as much as a Virginia "old field" is to a planter—has not even the solidity of "poor land," but vanishes away into a cloud of dust before the sweeping statement of the General Assembly, in these words: "The question, therefore, which this General Assembly is called upon to decide, is this: Do the Scriptures teach that the holding of slaves, *without regard to circumstances*, is a sin, the renunciation of which should be made a condition of membership in the Church of Christ?" p. 812. That was the point which the Assembly not only expressed in its own language, but decided by its last action, viz., that *circumstances* enter into the justification, or condemnation, of slaveholding.

It may be added that Dr. N. L. Rice, who drew up the Report, is not apt to use the contradictory of the language of abolitionists, unless it is the very best form to meet their fanaticism. There is not a particle of evidence from the records, however, to show that the Assembly merely followed the language of others. The four quotations *vary in form*, which is the best possible proof that the language is original and independent, whilst the idea of "circumstances" pervades the whole Report. Your "leafless tree" must, therefore, continue to remain in its withered state; for it receives neither light nor heat from the luminary of the General Assembly. Here are the four quotations referred to:

1. "The question, which is now unhappily agitating and dividing other branches of the Church, is, whether the holding of slaves is under all circumstances, a heinous sin, calling for the discipline of the Church."
2. "The question which this Assembly is called upon to decide is this: Do the Scriptures teach that the holding of slaves, without regard to circumstances, is a sin?"
3. "The Apostles did not denounce the relation itself as sinful."
4. "The Assembly cannot denounce the holding of slaves as necessarily a heinous and scandalous sin."

If the reader wishes to see how the uniform testimony of the General Assembly sustains my form of stating the doctrine (whilst it ignores that of Dr. Armstrong), he may find the record on page 41 of this Pamphlet.

SECTION IV.—DR. ARMSTRONG'S WEAPON TO DO BATTLE WITH.

I still think that your mode of stating the doctrine lacks the power of resisting abolitionism. Nor am I convinced of the contrary by the "fact" you adduce, which is, indeed, somewhat shadowy or indefinite. If we are to understand by the "fact,"

Dr. Hill's high estimate of your skill as a champion, it does not necessarily follow that, after seeing your statement of the doctrine, Dr. Hill should consider it the *best possible;* and if he should, I do not see that his opinion is more of "a fact" than mine. Or if the "fact" be that the two selected champions could not agree on the terms of the combat, I do not think this is a proof of skill on either side. Or if the "fact" be that, after you had put forth your argument, you gave your adversary the challenge to fight in the mode of your own choice, I do not think it a necessary and logical inference that his declination shows he considered your arguments, in all respects, unanswerable. And if he did, it is not clear that all other people should; or that my opinion should not have as much weight as that of a man who, for some reason or other, has not condescended to notice your excellent book at all. I deny, therefore, the correctness of your charge, that I have "compelled you to become a fool in glorying," because there has really been no occasion to glory.

Do not understand me as, in the least, disparaging your ability as a logician and controversialist. Far from it. No man, probably, in Virginia could sustain, with more plausibility and force, your defective proposition on slavery. But notwithstanding all this exhibition of your controversial skill, I believe it to be a "fact," that your proposition is "no weapon to do battle with." The statement that "slaveholding is not a sin in the sight of God," without reference to circumstances, has not the capacity to do full execution. As a cannon-ball with holes and cavities cannot be made to go straight, so your statement of doctrine zigzags away from the mark, in spite of all your propelling powers.

I have never doubted the purity of your intentions. But it is a singular development of human nature that men, who were born at the North, should generally be the warmest advocates of extravagant pro-slavery views. This is not said *in invidiam;* but as a simple rejoinder to your statement that, being born at the North, you had many prejudices to overcome, before reaching your present opinions. I do not doubt the truth of this latter statement.

SECTION V.—DR. ARMSTRONG ON SYLLOGISMS.

§ 1. Let us now turn again, from comparatively irrelevant matter, to the real point at issue. You have put your argument, with some show of triumph, into the form of a syllogism, and peremptorily call me to meet the argument "fairly and squarely," for "thus only can you [I] influence the opinions of thinking men:" p. 78. I accept the syllogistic form and the appeal to thinking men, and shall endeavour to show the weakness of your first and principal syllogism. The others require no notice, now. Your syllogism is as follows:

" A. Whatever Christ and his inspired Apostles refused to make a bar to communion, a court of Christ has no authority to make such.

"But, Christ and his inspired Apostles did refuse to make slaveholding a bar to communion.

"Therefore, a court of Christ has no authority to make slaveholding a bar to communion:" p. 76.

§ 2. In the first place, I deny the correctness of your logical view of the syllogism; and in the second place, I maintain that, even if the syllogism were faultless, it would not prove that my statement of the Scripture doctrine of slavery was wrong.

As to the syllogism, the error is in supposing that there are no circumstances, of any sort, in the premises. It is true that no circumstances, or qualifications, are introduced *expressly*, or in so many words; but they are *implied;* and, according to "a fundamental principle of logic," they are implied, to an equal extent, in the conclusion. I have shown, over and over again, that your own proposition, when analyzed, has reference to *some*, not to *all* slavery; and, therefore, that some circumstances are necessarily introduced. In your answer to the question whether your proposition "involves the idea that all slaveholding is sinless in the sight of God," you say, "By no means:" p. 6. And again, your proposition "can properly apply to such slaveholding only as subsists in conformity with the law of God:" p. 7. Now all such circumstances, that render slaveholding unlawful, are implied in the premise, and consequently in the conclusion. The resolution, adopted by the General Assembly, explicitly refers to circumstances in the general, undér which slavery exists in the United States. The Assembly's paper was formed in view of those circumstances, and they qualify the whole document.

It is perfectly clear that "circumstances" must be necessarily implied to some extent, in your syllogism, according to your theory of its meaning; and "circumstances" are involved in the conclusion by a "fundamental principle of logic."

§ 3. Admitting, however, that slaveholding, within the limits specified by yourself (which exclude the general circumstances connected with "well being" and the "public welfare," called by you "political"), cannot be made a bar to Church communion, what then? Does this prove that slaveholding does not become sinful, when "well being" and the "public welfare" require emancipation? Or does it prove that slaveholding may continue to exist without sin "until Christ's second coming?" By no means. Slaveholding may become sinful under circumstances in which it cannot be made the subject of Church discipline. It is just because slaveholding is right or wrong according to circumstances, that it is not allowed to become a bar to Church communion. Expediency cannot be made the ground of universal and perpetual obligation; and, therefore, things that in morals are classed among the *adiaphora* are not necessarily within the range of Church discipline. But are such things, therefore, innocent under all circumstances? Of course not. Their very nature implies the contrary. The fact that the Church is precluded, by the nature of the case, from disciplining persons, whose conduct is "right or *wrong* according to circumstances," does not acquit such persons of sin. They may be great sinners "in the sight of God," for holding their fellowmen in bondage under circumstances contrary to "well being" and the "public welfare;" although the Church, which cannot read the hearts of men, or decide upon the details covering every case, may be prevented from exercising discipline. Your syllogism, therefore, proves nothing.

As the proper jurisdiction of the Church comes up in your next Letter, I will reserve its further discussion for that occasion.

SECTION VI.—DR. ARMSTRONG EXPLAINING HIS PROPOSITION.

One of the most singular things in this controversy—which, I do not wonder, begins to assume to you the appearance of "a dark and bloody ground"—is that my friend, Dr. Armstrong, first declares that every proposition "should be so expressed" as to bear examination "apart from all explanations," and then feels himself compelled, at every point, to offer explanations. This necessity is inherent in the nature of your doctrinal statement, and its defectiveness is made manifest by your own rule. A proposition that needs continual explanations, must be either obscurely or illogically expressed. I think yours is both; and obscurely, because illogically.

§ 1. Your first explanation is uncalled for; because your proposition, faulty as it is, was never charged with sanctioning the "incidental evils of slavery."

In saying, with Dr. Spring, that "the bondage of the Hebrews partook of the character of apprenticeship rather than of rigorous servitude," reference was made to the *mode of treatment* under the two relations, without confounding their nature.

It seems that my good brother Armstrong is willing to adopt the phraseology, "Slaveholding, in itself considered, is not sinful," provided I will allow him to make an explanation that explains it away; but on all such explanations as causes it to mean, "slaveholding free from its incidental evils," I am constrained to put my *veto.* Your explanation makes the meaning to be, "slaveholding *in itself considered* is right, if the *circumstances* are right;" that is, "slaveholding, without regard to circumstances is right, if the circumstances are right!"

§ 2. Your proposition certainly seems to justify the permanence of slavery. Notwithstanding your protests and disclaimers, and although you mean not so, your doctrine establishes passive obedience and the perpetuity of despotism and slavery. You set forth, as an article of faith, binding the conscience, that we must obey the powers that be, and that despotism and slavery are not sins. You object to interpolating into these propositions any qualifying or limiting circumstances, and have written two elaborate Letters against it. You, indeed, believe that circumstances may make them wrong: p. 7. But, then, you believe this "upon the authority of reason," and therefore, as you hold, this belief does *not* bind the conscience. Whoever, then, under the most oppressive despotism contends for the right of revolution, or when a community has fairly outgrown the state in which slavery is otherwise than unjust, for emancipation, is contending for what does not bind any man's conscience; while the doctrine that despotism and slavery are no sins—to which you will not allow any limitation from circumstances to be applied—confronts him, and does bind his conscience. How, if this be so, can a conscientious man, in any "circumstances" undertake to withhold obedience from despots, and exercise the "right of revolution," or venture to promote emancipation?

§ 3. The proposition that "slaveholding is not a sin in the sight of God," is so broad as to appear to cover up many circumstances that make it wrong. As an abstract proposition, without any explanation,—and you say, it ought to be so clear as to dispense with explanations—it certainly seems to involve the consequences mentioned in one of my Letters. Some of your explanations, of course, relieve it from some of the objections; but not from all. As a moral rule for keeping the conscience in a healthful condition, it is peculiarly faulty. If the relation becomes a sinful one, whenever the circumstances of "well being" and the "public welfare" require its dissolution, how completely in the dark does your statement keep the moral agent! What you call the *scriptural* doctrine is only a part of the true doctrine, and it tends to lull the conscience under the professed guidance of revelation.

§ 4. Your objection to my proposition that it "acquits the slaveholding member of the Church by a sort of *whip and clear him* judgment," is as untenable as ever, notwithstanding your version of that expression. It seems, by the bye, that the expression, instead of meaning "strike first, and then acquit," means "acquit first, and then strike!" How my statement can be interpreted into Lynch-law, which, either way, means the same thing, I am at a loss to conjecture. Mine is, you perceive, the *exact contradictory* of the abolition doctrine. It, in fact, "whips" the abolitionist, whilst it "clears" the slaveholder, if "circumstances" are in his favour. Far be it from me to cast any odium upon my brethren at the South, who are faithfully endeavouring to do their duty in the midst of many trials and anxieties. "God bless them in their work of faith and labour of love," is the prayer of ten thousands of Christians at the North. I have honestly thought that my proposition affords to the conscientious slaveholder *a clearer vindication* than yours; and it is not encumbered with the difficulties and logical consequences, that press yours on every side.

§ 5. The last paragraph in your Letter is singularly out of place. In arguing against your statement, I attempted to show that the opinions, which you complain of my charging upon you, were "fairly involved" in that form of statement. A controversialist is not supposed to charge the obnoxious inferences as the opinions of his adversary, but rather, to take it for granted that he repudiates these opinions, and hence will be constrained to repudiate the doctrine that leads to them by legitimate consequences; or at all events, if not he, that the public, to whom the argument is also addressed, will repudiate it. However this may be, no one has a right to complain of an adversary for showing the evil consequences of his opinions. To object to the refutation of an argument by showing its false consequences, is to object to its being refuted at all.

SECTION VII.—THOUGHTS TOWARDS THE CLOSE.

§ 1. It is not at all unlikely that many "thinking men," who carefully consider our respective statements, will think the statement, "slaveholding is not necessarily and in all circumstances sinful" a much better one than "slaveholding is not a sin in the sight of God." My statement needs no explanations, whilst yours requires props on every side.

§ 2. Your suggestion of spending *ten* hours to my *one*, in considering the subject of slavery, is of no avail in an argument. Moral propositions depend upon being supported by truth, not time. There are some men, who are " always learning, and never able to come to a knowledge of the truth." This, of course, does not apply to yourself; especially, because you are so near the truth, that there is every reason to expect that you will soon reach it, in its perfection.

§ 3. Your complaint that our brethren at the South have been subjected to much misapprehension and obloquy by fanatical men at the North is unfortunately true. I deprecate this as much as you do. But a good degree of this abuse has been owing to the ultra defenders of slavery, whose unwarrantable statements and arguments have provoked a spirit of alienation and a fierce reaction both in sentiment and in opinion. The continuance of the peace of our Church depends, under God, upon the continuance of the moderation which has hitherto characterized our spirit, opinions, and measures.

§ 4. You say, " Let Mr. Barnes specify the *circumstances*, and I doubt whether even he would object to your statement:" p. 76. This is precisely what Mr. Barnes has no right to do for another man. He may form his own judgment of the case, and express it, and argue it, and endeavour to make all others receive it as true. But he cannot enforce his own views as a moral standard for others. As he admits that "Abraham's slaveholding was no sin," there is good reason to hope for candour, in general. But neither he, nor I, nor any other man, can make his own rule of morality, in matters that are *adiaphora*, to be *authority* for anybody else.

§ 5. You ask, why your statement sounds in my ears "like an old tune with unpleasant variations," and sung, you might have added, by the chorister almost alone, whilst Dr. Hodge's sounds like "Old Hundred," in which the whole congregation joins? I will tell you. Your form of statement is unknown to the General Assembly, from its organization down to the present time. You cannot point to a single sentence in all our Church testimonies that, rightly "said or sung," harmonizes with yours. Dr. Hodge, on the other hand, agrees with the General Assembly, whose form of statement is also adopted by your opponent. Dr. Hodge is in sympathy with *all* the deliverances of the General Assembly, whilst to many of them you carefully avoid allusion, in the very midst of the subject which invites an appeal to them; and even the testimony of 1845 you appear to desire to explain away, and to extract the very pith of doctrine from that majestic rod, that buds even like Aaron's.

§ 6. The eternal principles of justice, which are revealed in the Holy Scriptures, and are the reflection of the attributes of God, must decide the various questions relating to domestic servitude, and justify or condemn "according to circumstances." Whilst we both agree in the appeal to that tribunal, whose decision is "of record," happier is he who will be found at last to have interpreted that record aright, and to have exhibited the truth in nearest conformity to the Divine will!

I am yours, truly,
C. VAN RENSSELAER.

DR. VAN RENSSELAER'S SECOND REJOINDER.

EMANCIPATION AND THE CHURCH.*

TO THE REV. G. D. ARMSTRONG, D.D.:

Your second rejoinder discusses three subjects, 1. Emancipation and the Church. 2. Emancipation and the State, or Schemes of Emancipation. 3. The History of Anti-slavery Opinions.

The second subject is an entirely new one, which I have hitherto refrained from touching, and which, under ordinary circumstances, I should still decline to discuss.

SECTION I.—IS EMANCIPATION EXCLUSIVELY A POLITICAL QUESTION?

It has been my endeavour to discriminate carefully between the moral and political aspects of slavery, and to disclaim any inter-

* The course of remark pursued in this article, was determined chiefly by Dr. Armstrong's Rejoinder, to which it is a reply. The Scriptural argument is stated more particularly in my previous letters.

ference of the Church, with the proper work of the State. The State alone possesses the right to establish and enforce measures of general emancipation. But does legislation exhaust the subject? In my judgment, it does not. Emancipation has moral and religious relations, as well as political. No slaveholder has the moral right to keep his slaves in bondage, if they are prepared for freedom, and he can wisely set them free.*

1. There is a distinction between a moral end, to be kept in view, and the political means of attaining that end. The measures to secure emancipation may be political measures, but the end contemplated rests upon a moral obligation. It is my duty, as a Christian, to prepare my slaves for freedom, when Providence opens the way; and yet, I may be so restrained by State laws as to depend upon political intervention for a plan of emancipation. With the latter, the Church has nothing to do.

2. Slavery is not, like despotism, *enjoined* by law. Every individual may be a slaveholder or not, as he pleases. Here is an important distinction, which you entirely overlook. Whilst the State has the right to control emancipation, and can alone originate general measures, binding upon all its citizens, it commonly leaves emancipation to the discretion of the slaveholder himself. In Virginia, any person may emancipate his slaves, who makes provision for their removal out of the State. The act of emancipation, under these circumstances, is a lawful act of the master, which in no way interferes with politics. Where shall a person thus situated, whose conscience troubles him, go for direction? To the State? To the members of the Legislature? No! The question is one of duty to his God. It involves a religious and moral principle; and, admitting that his slaves are prepared for freedom, it is outside of politics. The slaveholder must search the Scriptures, or he may consult the testimonies of the Church for her interpretation of the Scriptures. The Church has a perfect right to give to her members advice on this subject which will guide them in perplexity; and this advice may be volunteered, if circumstances seem to demand it.

3. Slaves stand, ecclesiastically, in the relation of children to parents. Our General Assembly has declared that Christian masters, who have the right to bring their children to baptism, may also present for baptism, in their own name, the children of their slaves. Can it be conceived that the Church has no right to counsel her members concerning the nature and continuance of this peculiar relationship throughout her own households?

4. Slaveholding is "right or wrong, according to circumstances." It belongs in morals to the *adia·⁷·*   things indifferent. It may be right in 1858, and wrong _   ₋ₒ, according as the slaves may be not prepared, or prepared, for emancipation. The very

---

* A fair compensation may be claimed for the pecuniary sacrifice involved in manumission, either from the State or from the slaves themselves.

nature of the class of subjects to which it belongs, places it within the scope of church testimony. The continuance or discontinuance of slaveholding, concerns the character of the slaveholder as a righteous man.

5. Even if the State should altogether remove emancipation from the power of the individual slaveholder, and determine to exercise exclusive jurisdiction over the matter, what then? In the first place, the obligation would still rest upon the master to elevate his slaves, and to set them free whenever the way was open. And in the second place, the master would be bound, as a citizen, to exert himself to obtain from the State the necessary public measures to secure at the right time the same object.

Emancipation is not "properly a political question" in any sense that makes it cease to be a moral and religious one. So far as it partakes of the latter character, the Church has a right, within the limits of her authority, to utter her testimony in favour of it.

SECTION II.—SLAVERY AND THE INTERESTS OF THE LIFE TO COME.

One of your arguments for excluding emancipation from the influence of Church testimony is that "it does not immediately concern the interests of the life to come." This point can best be determined by impartial witnesses, personally acquainted with the practical workings of slavery. Allow me, then, in all courtesy, to introduce the testimony of some of the ablest and most respected ministers of the Presbyterian Church, who are familiar with the system in its best forms. A Committee, appointed by the Synod of Kentucky, made a Report to that body, in 1835, in which they characterized the system of slavery in the following manner:

"There are certain *effects* springing naturally and necessarily out of such a system, which must also be considered.

"1. Its most striking effect is, *to deprave and degrade its subjects by removing from them the strongest natural checks to human corruption.* There are certain principles of human nature by which God works to save the moral world from ruin. In the slave these principles are eradicated. He is degraded to a mere creature of appetite and passion. These are the feelings by which he is governed. The salt which preserves human nature is extracted, and it is left a putrefying mass.

"2. *It dooms thousands of human beings to hopeless ignorance.* The slave has no motive to acquire knowledge. The master will not undergo the expense of his education. The law positively forbids it. Nor can this state of things become better unless it is determined that slavery shall cease. Slavery cannot be perpetuated if education be generally or universally given to slaves.

"3. *It deprives its subjects, in a great measure, of the privileges of the Gospel.* Their inability to read prevents their access to the Scriptures. The Bible is to them a sealed book. There is no adequate provision made for their attendance upon the public means of grace. Nor are they prepared to profit from instructions designed for their masters.

They listen when in the sanctuary to prophesyings in an unknown tongue. Comparatively few of them are taught to bow with their masters around the domestic altar. Family ordinances of religion are almost unknown in the domestic circles of the blacks.

"4. *This system licenses and produces great cruelty.* The whip is placed in the hands of the master, and he may use it at his pleasure, only avoiding the destruction of life. Slaves often suffer all that can be inflicted by wanton caprice, by grasping avarice, by brutal lust, by malignant spite, and by insane anger. Their happiness is the sport of every whim, and the prey of every passion that may enter the master's bosom. Their bodies are lacerated with the lash. Their dignity is habitually insulted. Their tenderest affections are wantonly crushed. Dearest friends are torn asunder. Brothers and sisters, parents and children, see each other no more. There is not a neighbourhood where these heart-rending scenes are not displayed. There is not a village or a road that does not behold the sad procession of manacled outcasts, whose chains and mournful countenances tell that they are exiled by force from all they hold dear.

"5. *It produces general licentiousness among the slaves.* Marriage, as a civil ordinance, they cannot enjoy. Their marriages are mere contracts, voidable at their master's pleasure or their own: And never, in any civilized country, has respect for these restraints of matrimony been more nearly obliterated than it has been among our blacks. This system of universal concubinage produces revolting licentiousness.

"6. *This system demoralizes the whites as well as the blacks.* The masters are clothed with despotic power. To depraved humanity this is exceedingly dangerous. Indolence is thus fostered: And hard-heartedness, selfishness, arrogance, and tyranny are, in most men, rapidly developed and fearfully exhibited.

"7. *This system draws down upon us the vengeance of Heaven.* 'If thou forbear to deliver them that are drawn to death, and those that are ready to be slain; if thou sayest, Behold, we knew it not; doth not he that pondereth the heart consider it? and he that keepeth thy soul, doth he not know it? and shall he not render to every man according to his works?' 'The people of the land have used oppression, and exercised robbery, and have vexed the poor and needy; yea, they have oppressed the stranger wrongfully. . . . Therefore have I poured out mine indignation upon them: I have consumed them with the fire of my wrath; their own way have I recompensed upon their heads, saith the Lord.' Such is the system, such are some of its effects."

The right of the Church to testify against the permanence of a system of this character, cannot be resisted by pointing to the overruling providence of God, through which many slaves have been brought into his kingdom. The Bible, it is true, treats the distinctions of this life as of comparatively little consequence, and enjoins submission even to wrong-doing and persecution. But must the Church, therefore, refrain from testifying against all social and moral evils, and from exhorting her members to use their best endeavours to bring them to an end?

The two facts adduced by you, do not prove that the Church has no interest in emancipation. 1. In regard to the number of church members among the slaves, I deny that "a larger proportion of the labouring classes belong to the Christian Church where the labourers are chiefly slaves, than in the Northern States, where slavery does not exist."

2. Your second fact, that the number of church members among the slaves, is nearly double the number of communicants in the heathen world, proves that God has overruled the system of slavery for good, but not that the Church has no interest in its abrogation. When we consider that at least fifteen thousand ministers of the Gospel live in the Slave States, being in the proportion of one minister to seven hundred of the whole population, while, on the other hand, the number of missionaries among the heathen is only in the proportion of one minister to three hundred thousand of the population, the comparison by no means exalts slavery as an instrument of evangelization. Look, rather, for a better example to the Sandwich Islands, where society has been Christianized in a single generation.

The system of slavery, as appears from the analysis of its evils by our Kentucky brethren, has so many and immediate connections with the life to come, that the Christian Church may wisely testify in favour of its abrogation, as a lawful end, whenever Providence opens the way for it.

SECTION III.—SLAVERY AND THE BIBLE.

The Word of God, when fairly interpreted, contains much instruction upon this subject. In the first place, the exhortation of Paul to the slaves is: "Art thou called, being a servant? Care not for it. BUT IF THOU MAYST BE FREE, USE IT RATHER." (1 Cor. 7 : 21.) This last declaration proves that slavery is not a natural and permanent condition ; that liberty is a higher and better state than bondage ; and that emancipation is an object of lawful desire to the slaves, and a blessing which Christian masters may labour to confer upon them. In endeavouring to escape the power of this apostolic declaration, you maintain that it has only a local application, and that "throughout the chapter, in answer to inquiries from the Church at Corinth, Paul is giving instruction with especial regard to the circumstances in which the Corinthians were placed at that time, and hence, every special item of advice must be interpreted with this fact in view." The same thing is stated in your book.

1. Admitting your *local* interpretation to be the true one, what then? Does not my good brother Armstrong see that, if he in this way gets rid of Paul's declaration in favour of freedom, he also impairs the permanent obligation of Christian slaves to remain contented in their bondage ? If the *second* clause of the sentence has a local application, and is limited to the state of things in the Corinthian Church, is not the *first* clause limited by the same conditions ?

2. Again. The Apostle, in this chapter, carefully discriminates between what he speaks by "permission" and what by "commandment;" and it is strange logic that, because some passages, before and after the 21st verse, are of limited application, therefore every verse in the chapter is so. All that relates to virgins, and to the temporary avoidance of matrimony, &c., is declared to be merely advisory, in view of the existing state of things, or "the present distress;" whereas, the exhortation to believers to be contented with their external condition, from v. 17 to v. 24, is spoken by Divine authority; "and so ordain I in *all the churches*," v. 17. The whole of the passage, 17—24, is manifestly an authoritative declaration of inspiration.

3. Your reasoning in regard to 1 Cor. 7 : 21 would be much more to the purpose, if the hypothesis were that persons were *compelled by law* to enter into the marriage state, or to marry particular individuals. This would be analogous, in the most material points, to the case of the slaves. Surely, if one might be free from such compulsion, he ought to choose it rather, and that not only in apostolic times, but in every age.

Neither your incorrect interpretation nor your incongruous illustration weakens the force of Paul's famous declaration in favour of freedom, as the best social condition and one that may rightfully be kept in view. Dr. Hodge says, *in loco*, "Paul's object is not to exhort men not to improve their condition, but simply not to allow their social relations to disturb them. He could, with perfect consistency with the context, say, 'Let not your being a slave give you any concern; but if you can become free, choose freedom rather than slavery.'" If the Church, following Paul's example, can give this exhortation to slaves, she can at least exhort and advise masters to take measures to prepare their slaves for freedom, whenever Providence shall open the way for its blessings.

I have not rested the right of the Church to keep emancipation in view, simply upon this single text, but I have showed that, not only do "the universal spirit and principles of religion originate and foster sentiments favourable to the natural rights of mankind," but that "the injunctions of Scripture to masters tend to and necessarily terminate in emancipation." "If the Scriptures enjoin what, of necessity, leads to emancipation, they enjoin emancipation, when the time comes; if they forbid what is necessary to the perpetuity of slavery, they forbid that slavery should be perpetuated." "The Church, therefore, may scripturally keep in view this great moral result, to the glory of her heavenly King." (See *Letters*.)

SECTION IV.—THINGS THAT AVAIL, OR AVAIL NOT.

1. You remind me that "it will avail nothing to show that *the Church has often made deliverances on the subject in years that are passed*," and that "political preaching" and "political church-deliverances" date back "from the days of Constantine," when

Church and State became united. Here is an ingenious attempt to dishonour history, and to beat down ancient, as well as modern, testimony. 1. You seem to admit, on reconsideration, that the general testimony of the Church, from the days of Constantine, is against the perpetuity of slavery. 2. But how do you account for the fact that the General Assembly of our Church, which, from its very organization, has been *free* from State dominion, has uniformly testified in favour of preparing the slaves for liberty? On referring to your rejoinder, I find this aberration accounted for on the ground that our Church has not had time to "fully comprehend her true position!" A monarchist might say that, for the same reason, our fathers prematurely drew up the Declaration of Independence, not having waited long enough to comprehend the true position of their country! How much time, beyond *half a century*, does it take the Presbyterian Church to define her interpretation of the word of God? The last deliverance of the General Assembly, in 1845, was affirmed by that body to be harmonious with the first deliverance in 1787. Fifty-eight years produced no variation of sentiment. This uniform testimony of the highest judicatory of the Church must naturally possess great weight, or will "avail" much, with every true Presbyterian.*

2. You add, "Nor will it avail to show that *emancipation has a bearing upon the well-being of a people—even their spiritual well-being.*" I am truly glad to obtain from Dr. Armstrong this incidental and gratuitous admission, that emancipation really has a bearing upon the best interests of the human family. I thank my good brother for it; although he immediately attempts to nullify it by the declaration that "commerce, railways, agriculture, manufactures," &c., which also promote the welfare of society, cannot, simply on that account, become the subjects of ecclesiastical concern. Our Foreign Missionary Board might certainly build or charter a vessel, if necessary; and it actually sends out printers to work presses, farmers to till the soil, and physicians to minister to bodily health. On the same principle, it might send out "bells" for the mission churches, or even cast them in "foundries," if bells were of sufficient importance, and could not be otherwise obtained. But the principle on which the Church testifies in favour of emancipation is, that it is a moral duty to set slaves free, when prepared in God's providence for freedom; and if the performance of a moral duty has "a bearing upon the well-being of a people," must it therefore be set aside?

3. You also state that it will avail nothing in this argument,

---

* If Dr. Baxter was a "wiser man" "eighteen years" after 1818, and was therefore entitled to the consideration of higher wisdom in 1836, then still higher wisdom is due to the General Assembly, in 1846, when that body reaffirmed the testimony of 1818, *twenty-eight* years after the issuing of their great document.

I have yet to learn that Dr. Baxter changed his views on the subject of slavery. At least, no quotation of his sentiments by Dr. Armstrong proves it. I have sought in vain for a copy of Dr. Baxter's pamphlet. Will any friend present a copy to the Presbyterian Historical Society? C. V. R.

unless I can show that *you "place emancipation in the wrong category, or that the Church has a right to meddle with politics."* This is going over ground already discussed. Let me say, again, that the exhortation of the Church to keep emancipation as an end in view, does not prescribe either the mode or the time of emancipation, and does not in any way come in conflict with the State ; and the Church does not "meddle with politics," when she concerns herself about moral duties. If it be a moral duty for a Christian to elevate his slaves and to set them free, when prepared for freedom, the Church has a right to make that declaration, provided she thinks it fairly deducible from the spirit, principles, and precepts of the word of God.

SECTION V.—A NEW QUESTION! POLITICS. SCHEMES OF EMAN-
CIPATION. COLONIZATION, ETC.

The largest part of your Rejoinder is taken up with new matter, which is foreign to the discussion of "Emancipation and the Church," and which, according to law, is irrelevant in a Rejoinder, the nature of which is an answer to a previous Replication. I regret that you have *insisted* upon opening this new field of discussion ; but, believing that your remarks leave wrong impressions upon the mind of the reader, I shall take advantage of the occasion to throw out suggestions from a different stand-point.

SECTION VI.—POPULAR ERRORS.

I propose, without finding fault with some of the popular errors on your list, to add to their number. I do this, in order to present additional and true elements which belong to the solution of this intricate and difficult problem.

I. It is a mistake to suppose that *the slaves have not a natural desire for freedom*, however erroneous may be their views of freedom. There are certain natural impulses which belong to man, by the constitution of his being. No slavery can quench the aspirings for liberty. In the language of the late GOVERNOR MC-DOWELL, one of your old fellow-citizens, at Lexington, and one of Virginia's noblest sons, "Sir, you may place the slave where you please ; you may dry up to your uttermost the fountains of his feelings, the springs of his thought ; you may close upon his mind every avenue of knowledge, and cloud it over with artificial night ; you may yoke him to your labours as the ox which liveth only to work, and worketh only to live ; you may put him under any process, which, without destroying his value as a slave, will debase and crush him as a rational being ; you may do this, and the idea that he was born to be free will survive it all. It is allied to his hope of immortality—it is the ethereal part of his nature, which oppression cannot rend. It is a torch lit up in his soul by the hand of the Deity, and never meant to be extinguished by the hand of man."

If the desire of the slaves for freedom be not as intelligent as it might be, the excuse lies partly in the want of opportunities to acquire higher knowledge, and partly in the bad example of idleness set by the free blacks and by the whites. And if the privilege of liberty were granted in society only to those who entertained entirely correct views of its nature, how many thousands of free citizens in this, and in all lands, ought to be reduced to slavery? It deserves to be remarked in all candour, and without disparagement, that there is danger of the prevalence, in a slave-holding community, of an unintelligent estimate of the value of future liberty to the slaves.

II. It is a mistake to suppose that *slaves possess no natural rights*. Their present incapacity to "exercise beneficially these rights" does not destroy the title to them, but only suspends it. In the mean time, the slaves possess the correlative right of *being made prepared* for the equal privileges of the whole family of man.

Your remarks that slavery secures to the slaves the right to labour in a better way "than it is secured to a more elevated race of labourers in Europe, under any of the systems which prevail among the civilized nations of the Old World," will hardly be received by autocrats and despots as a plea for reviving slavery on the continent. Indeed, the new Emperor, Alexander of Russia, is engaged, at this very time, in the great work of doing homage to Christian civilization by emancipating all the serfs of the empire.

III. Another error consists in regarding the Africans *as an inferior race, fit only to be slaves*. Infidelity, as you are aware, has been active at the South in inducing the belief that the negro belongs to an inferior, if not a distinct race. This doctrine is the only foundation of perpetual slavery.* It is alike hostile to emancipation and injurious to all efforts to elevate the negro to his true position as a fellow-man and an immortal. The slaves belong to Adam's race; are by nature under the wrath and curse, even as others; subjects of the same promises; partakers of the same blessings in Jesus Christ, and heirs of the same eternal inheritance. How the last great day will dissipate unscriptural and inhuman prejudices against these children of the common brotherhood!

IV. It is an error to suppose that *slavery is not responsible for suffering, vice, and crime, prevalent under its dominion*. Even were the slaves, if set free, to degenerate into a lower condition, slavery cannot escape from the responsibility of being an abettor of many injuries and evils. Much of the vice and crime of the manufacturing districts of England is undoubtedly owing to that system of labour, which thus becomes responsible for it. According to your theory, it would seem that no system of social or political

---

* This defence of perpetual slavery is as old as Aristotle. That philosopher, wishing to establish some plausible plea for slavery, says, " *The barbarians are of a different race from us, and were born to be slaves to the Greeks.*" To use the language of chess, this doctrine is "Aristotle's opening."

despotism is accountable for the darkness and degradation of the people. It is sin that causes all the maladies of slavery! But is there no connection between slavery and sin, as demonstrated by the experience of ages? Is slavery a system so innocent as to cast off the obligation to answer for all the suffering and wickedness that have been perpetrated under its connivance? Far be it from me to deny whatever good has been accomplished, in divine Providence, through human bondage. God brings good out of evil; but I cannot shut my eyes to the conviction that slavery is directly responsible to God for a large amount of iniquity, both among the whites and the blacks, which, like a dark cloud, is rolling its way to the judgment.

V. It is an error to suppose that *the African slave-trade ought to be revived.* Among all the popular errors of the day, this is the most mischievous and wicked. God denounces the traffic in human flesh and blood. It has the taint of murder. Our national legislation righteously classes it with piracy, and condemns its abettors to the gallows. And yet, in Conventions and Legislatures of a number of the slave-holding States, the revival of the African slave-trade meets with favour. This fact is an ominous proof of the demoralization of public sentiment, under the influence and operation of a system of slavery.

VI. Another error is, that *slavery is a permanent institution.* Slavery in the United States must come to an end. Christianity is arraying the public opinion of the world against it. The religion of Jesus Christ never has, and never can countenance the perpetuity of human bondage. The very soil of the planting States, which is growing poorer and poorer every year, refuses to support slavery in the long run. Its impoverished fields are not often renovated, and the system must in time die the death of its own sluggish doom. Besides, the competition of free labour must add to the embarrassments of slavery. Even Africa herself may yet contend with the slave productions of America, in the market of the world.

In short, slavery is compelled to extinction by the operation of natural laws in the providence of the everliving God—which laws act in concert with the spirit and principles of his illuminating word.

VII. Another popular delusion is, that *slavery will always be a safe system.* Thus far, the African race has exhibited extraordinary docility. Will this submission endure forever? God grant that it may! But who, that has a knowledge of human nature, does not tremble in view of future insurrections, under the newly devised provocations of reviving the slave-trade, banishing the free blacks from the soil, and prohibiting emancipation? Granting that insurrections will be always suppressed in the end, yet what terrific scenes of slaughter may they enact on a small scale; what terror will they carry into thousands of households; and what hatred and enmity will they provoke between the two races! The future of slavery in America will present, in all probability, a dark and gloomy history, unless our beloved brethren exert themselves, in season, to arrest its progress, and to provide for its extinction.

The prevalent sentiment in Virginia, in 1832, was thus uttered in the Legislature by *Mr. Chandler, of Norfolk:* "It is admitted by all who have addressed this house, that slavery is a curse, and an increasing one. That it has been destructive to the lives of our citizens, history, with unerring truth, will record. That its future increase will create commotion, cannot be doubted."

VIII. Another mistake is, that *nothing can be done for the removal of slavery.* Elevation is the grand demand of any, and every, scheme of emancipation. Can nothing more be done for the intellectual and moral elevation of the slaves? Much is, indeed, already in process of accomplishment; but this work is left rather to individual Christian exertion, than to the benevolent operation of public laws. The laws generally discourage education, and thus disown the necessity of enlarged measures for intellectual improvement. If it be said that education and slavery are inconsistent with each other, the excuse is proof of the natural tendency of the system to degradation. Who will deny, however, that a great deal more might be done to prepare the slaves for freedom by private effort and by public legislation? Can it be doubted that measures, favouring prospective emancipation, might be wisely introduced into many of the Slave States? If there were, first, a willing mind, could there not be found, next, a practicable way? PHILIP A. BOLLING, of Buckingham, declared in the Virginia Legislature, in 1832, "The day is fast approaching, when those who oppose all action on this subject, and instead of aiding in devising some feasible plan for freeing their country from an acknowledged curse, cry '*impossible*' to every plan suggested, will curse their perverseness and lament their folly." This is strong language. It comes from one of the public men of your own State, and is adapted to awaken thought.

IX. The last popular error I shall specify, is, that *none of the slaves are now prepared for freedom.* Whilst I am opposed to a scheme of immediate and universal emancipation, for reasons that need not be stated, I suppose that a large number of slaves are capable of rising at once to the responsibilities of freedom, under favouring circumstances, for example, in Liberia. Probably Norfolk itself could furnish scores of such persons, or, to keep within bounds, one score. There must be thousands throughout the plantations of the South, who are, in a good degree, prepared to act well their part in free and congenial communities. Such a representation honours the civilizing power of slavery, and has an important bearing on schemes of emancipation.

SECTION VII.—SCHEMES OF EMANCIPATION.

I am now prepared to follow your example in offering some remarks on "emancipation laws."

Allow me here to repeat my regret that you have persisted in discussing this subject. First, because it is foreign to the topic of "Emancipation and the Church;" secondly, because the discussion involves speculations rather than principles; and thirdly, because no living man can, on the one side or the other, deliver very clear utterances, especially without more study than I, for one, have been able to give to the subject. Good, however, will result from an interchange of opinions. My chief motive in noticing this new part of your Rejoinder, on emancipation, is an unwillingness to allow your pro-slavery views to go forth in this Magazine without an answer.

You are right, I think, in supposing that the best emancipation scheme practicable would embrace the following particulars:

"(1.) A law prospective in its operation—say that all slaves born after a certain year, shall become free at the age of twenty-five.

"(2.) Provision for the instruction of those to be emancipated in the rudiments of learning.

"(3.) Provision for their transfer and comfortable settlement in Africa, when they become free."

Your *first objection* to this scheme is that, "in its practical working, it would prove, to a very large extent, a *transportation*, and not an *emancipation* law." Let us look at this objection.

1. Many owners of slaves would go with them into other States, and thus no injury would be inflicted upon the slaves, whilst the area of freedom behind them would be enlarged.

2. Many masters would make diligent and earnest efforts to prepare their slaves for freedom, on their plantations, even if other masters sold their slaves for transportation.

3. If some, or many, of the masters were to sell their slaves, it would be doing no more than is done in Virginia, at the present time. The number of Virginia slaves transported annually into other States, has been estimated as high as fifty thousand.

4. A compensation clause might be attached to the plan we are considering, with a prohibition against transportation.

5. The objection is founded upon the supposition that only some of the States adopted the emancipation scheme. The objection would also be diminished in force, in proportion to the number of States adopting the scheme, because the supply of slaves may become greater than the demand.

6. Some evils, necessarily attendant upon general schemes of emancipation, are more than counterbalanced by the greater good accomplished. If Delaware, Maryland, VIRGINIA, Kentucky, Tennessee, and Missouri, were to adopt a scheme of prospective emancipation,* the general advantage to those States, in a social, moral, intellectual, and economical point of view, would more than counterbalance the inherent and minor evils incident to the scheme.

* Ought not such a scheme to *begin* with these States?

The addition of six new States to the area of freedom would probably outweigh all the trials incident to the transition period.

An emancipation scheme, similar to that propounded, was tested in the Northern States, where it succeeded well; and you còuld not have appealed to a better illustration of its wisdom. The number of slaves transported could not have been very great, because the whole number in New England, New York, New Jersey, and Pennsylvania, was only about 40,000 in the year 1790, when these schemes were generally commenced, and the number of Africans in those States was more than double at the next census.

On the whole, a prospective emancipation scheme, with or without a compensation or prohibitory clause, would, in the States named, do more, in the end, in behalf of the African race and the cause of freedom, than the inactive policy of doing nothing.

Objection 2d. You object to the plan "on the ground that the slave race cannot be prepared for freedom by any short course of education, such as that proposed."

1. Suppose that the Legislature of Virginia should enact that all slaves born after 1870, shall become free at the age of twenty-five. The course of education would be precisely as long as the process of nature allows. It would embrace *the whole of the training period of an entire generation;* and with the intellectual and moral resources already in possession of the African race in Virginia, a general and faithful effort to elevate the young would result, under God, in a substantial advancement of condition, auguring well for freedom.

2. Your own experiment with the two slaves is just in point. It shows how much can be done, on a small scale, and, if so, on a larger scale. These slaves were taught to read and write; they were fitted for freedom at the age of thirty-two; and they were then set free, as "good colonists for Liberia." Although they did not ultimately go to Liberia, perhaps their addition "to the number of free negroes in Virginia," was esteemed by them a higher benefit than it seems to you. They were, at any rate, qualified for freedom in Liberia.

3. To the idea that all the emancipated slaves ought to be "compelled to go to Liberia," you present three difficulties. (1.) "It is vain to expect to make good citizens for Liberia, by sending them there against their will, like convicts to a penal colony." I reply, that Liberia is becoming to the African race more and more an object of desire; that there is no more compulsion in the case than their own best interests demands, as persons who, up to that period, are in the state of minors; that the prospect of liberty in Liberia is very different from that of penal labour and suffering by convicts; and that, if your remark be true, that it is vain to expect to make "good citizens for Liberia, by sending them against their will," is it not equally vain to expect to make good citizens of slaves by keeping them in slavery "against their will?" (2.)

You say that we deceive ourselves in speaking of Africa as "their native country," "their home." I reply that the race-mark indelibly identifies the slaves with Africa; that their own traditions connect them with their fatherland; that the decisions of the United States Supreme Court deny them to be "citizens" of this country; and that their own affections are becoming stronger and stronger in favour of returning to Africa, as their minds become enlightened. (3.) Another obstacle to "compulsory expatriation," in your judgment, is, that it would "sunder ties both of family and affection." I reply, not necessarily either the one or the other, as a general rule. On the supposition of a compensation law, which is the true principle, there would be no sundering of family ties; and as to ties of affection for their masters or friends left behind, every emigrant to our Western States expects to bear them. Besides, instead of a "compulsory expatriation," it would be virtually a voluntary return to the land of their fathers.

Objection 3d. Your third objection to the proposed gradual emancipation scheme is, that you "do not see the least prospect of Liberia being able to do the part assigned to it in this plan for a long time to come." This is the only objection of any real weight.

SECTION VIII.—LIBERIAN COLONIZATION.

You will agree with me, if I mistake not, in three particulars:

1. African Colonization is a scheme, founded in wise and far-reaching views of African character and destiny. The coloured race can never attain to social and political elevation in the United States. The experience of the past is a demonstration against the continuance of the two races in this country on terms favourable to the negroes; and there is reason to believe that the future will be a period of increased disadvantage and hardship. The colonization of the coloured people in Africa is, therefore, in its conception, a scheme of profound wisdom and true benevolence.

2. You will also agree with me in the opinion that the measures for Liberian Colonization may be *indefinitely extended.* Territory, larger than the Atlantic slope, may be procured in the interior of Africa; money enough may be obtained from the sale of the public lands, or from other national resources; vessels are already on hand to meet the demands of the largest transportation; and emigrants, of a hopeful character, and in large numbers, may be expected to present themselves, at the indicated time, in the providence of God. There are no limits to the plan of Liberian Colonization. Your own faith in its ultimate capabilities seems to be shaded with doubt, only in reference to the question of *time.*

3. Further. You will agree with me in the opinion that *much more might be done, at once,* in the actual working of the Liberian scheme. Among the coloured population in this country are large

numbers, both bond and free, who are superior to the average class of emigrants already sent out.

SECTION IX.—WHICH CLASS SHOULD BE SENT FIRST, THE FREE, OR THE SLAVES?

In your judgment, we ought " to adhere to the course marked out by the founders of the Colonization Society, and attend first to the free people of colour; and only after our work here has been done, ought we to think of resorting to colonization as an adjunct to emancipation."

1. The discussion of this issue is outside even of the new theme; because the plan of emancipation, proposed by yourself, *assumes* the colonization of the slaves as one of its main features. I submit that it is not in order to deny your own admissions.

2. The colonization of slaves, when set free, is precisely in accordance with the constitution of the American Colonization Society. And the Society has been acting upon this principle from the beginning. The majority of emigrants belong to the class that were once slaves, and who have been made free with the object of removal to Africa, as colonists.

3. I see no reason why the sympathy of philanthropy should be first concentrated upon the free blacks. This class of our population are, indeed, entitled to our warm interest and our Christian exertions to promote their welfare; but why to an exclusive and partial benevolence? If you reply, as you do, because "the condition of the free people of colour is worse than that of our slaves," then I beg leave to call in question the statement, and to invalidate it, in part, by your own declaration, that at least fifty thousand of the free blacks are more intelligent and better prepared for colonization than can be found among the slaves. When the exigency of the argument requires you to sustain slavery, you depreciate the free blacks and make them "lower than the slaves;" but when colonization demands the best quality of emigrants, then you depreciate the slaves and point to "fifty thousand" free blacks, who are superior to slaves.

4. I might assign many reasons why, if Liberian colonization be a benevolent scheme, the race in slavery ought not to be excluded from its benefits. But, this point being assumed, as I have stated, an axiom of our problem, it is unnecessary to establish it by argument.

5. Let us compromise this issue on a principle of Christian equity, viz.: *simultaneous* efforts should be made to colonize the blacks who are already free, and those who may be set free for that purpose. You will not deny that there are hundreds and thousands of Christian slaves who, if emancipated, would make good citizens of Liberia. Why, then, should the social and political elevation of these men be postponed, and the good they might do in Africa be

lost, simply because there are free people of colour in the land, who are also proper subjects of colonization?

SECTION X.—WHAT THE COLONIZATION SOCIETY HAS DONE.

Before the establishment of the Republic of Liberia, the future of the African race, in this country, was dreary and almost without hope. The mind of the philanthropist had no resting-place for its anxious thoughts; the pious slave-holder lived in faith, without the suggestion of any effectual remedy; and the negro race in America seemed doomed to labour for generations, and then sink away or perish. In God's good time, a Republic springs up in the Eastern world! It is an African Republic; and composed mainly of those who once were slaves in America. What an event in the history of civilization! Even in this last half century of wonders, it stands out in the greatness of moral and political pre-eminence.

For some account of the results of African Colonization, I refer you to my Address at the opening of the Ashmun Institute, entitled "GOD GLORIFIED BY AFRICA." It is sufficient here to say that the Liberian Republic, with its institutions of freedom, contains about 10,000 emigrants from America, of whom 6000 were once Southern slaves. Its schools, academies, and churches; its growing commerce, improving agriculture, and intelligent legislation; its favourable location, Protestantism, and Anglo-Saxon speech: all conspire to demonstrate the truth of the principles on which it was founded, and to develope a national prosperity rarely equalled in the history of colonization.

In short, the Liberian Republic is a *good work, well done.* LAUS DEO!

SECTION XI.—WHAT MAY BE REASONABLY EXPECTED OF LIBERIA.

Let us be hopeful. Cheer up, Brother Armstrong! Ethiopia is yet to stretch out her hands unto God. An eminent Southern divine has well said, "I acknowledge the duty, which rests upon all, to hope great things and attempt great things, and look with holy anxiety at the signs of the times."

I. Let us *hope* great things. "Hope, that is seen, is not hope;" and I may add, without irreverence, hope, that will not see, is not hope. Your views about the permanence of slavery prevent the access to your mind of large hopes from the Liberian scheme. In your Letters and Rejoinders, you several times express doubt whether slavery in the United States is ever to end! Nor does it seem to you very desirable that it should end.

II. The people of God should *attempt* great things for the African race. Prosperity has attended African colonization thus far; and under circumstances to stimulate to more active and extended efforts.

1. *Assimilation.* The great obstacle is, as you state, "the difficulty in assimilating such an immigration as we are able to send" to Liberia.

The fact of an "indiscriminate immigration," composed chiefly of slaves, accomplishing so much in Liberia, is very encouraging in regard to the possibility of success on a larger scale.

The emigrants to be sent out by the scheme of emancipation under review, would be of a higher character than the class already there. One of the features of this plan involves " provision for the *instruction* of those to be emancipated in the rudiments of learning." Education is, under God, a mighty elevator. The question, whether a people shall be raised up in the scale of intelligence or be allowed to remain unlettered and in gross ignorance, decides the destiny of nations. It will certainly decide the destiny of African colonization. The proposed plan contemplates a long interval of preparation, an interval of *thirty-seven years*, during which time a new generation is to come forward under a full system of "Christian appliances." A very different class of emigrants will, therefore, be made ready for colonization. Nor is it chimerical to suppose that great elevation of character would attend measures for the instruction of the young slaves, under the kindly intercourse, supervision, and example of one and a quarter millions of white members of the Church of Christ, and fifteen thousand ministers of the Gospel.* These emigrants, thus prepared for freedom, would be prepared for assimilation.

The difficulty of foreign immigration to this country is in its diversity and irreligion. Speaking foreign tongues, trained to different habits and customs, debased by Roman superstition, or corrupted by German infidelity, the mass of our immigrants are far more difficult to fuse into our existing population than would be the Africans *into their own race* at Liberia. In the case of colonization in Liberia, the population would be homogeneous, of a more intelligent order than the original population, and under the influences of the Christian religion.

African character is improving in Liberia. Instead of deteriorating, as when in contact with the white race, it is now gaining admiration in the political world. What has been wanting to raise the negro character is education, the habit of self-reliance, and a fair opportunity for development on a field of its own, unhindered by contact with the white race. An illustration of the elevating power of a removal to a congenial field, is seen in the case of thousands of impoverished whites in the slaveholding States. This class, doomed to poverty, and often to degradation, by the law of slavery, rise to influence, wealth, and importance, when they emi-

* This is the best estimate I can make of the number of white communicants and ministers in the Southern churches.

grate to new States. A similar influence will bless the negro race, when separated from contaminating influences, and disciplined to bear its part among the governments of the world.

In Liberia, new communities would be formed, and settlements established in different parts of the extending republic, to meet the demands of emigration. "Assimilation" is easier under circumstances of diffusion than of aggregation. As, in our own country, the facility of acquiring land in the new Territories and States, promotes the welfare of the emigrants, and fixes them in homes comparatively remote from cities and overgrown districts, so the Liberian scheme proposes to establish its large accessions of emigrants in independent and separate communities, increasing in number with the demand for enlargement.

2. The " deep-rooted *distrust* of the capacity of their own people for safely conducting the affairs of government" need give a friend of colonization no concern whatever. The race in this country has never had the opportunity of proving its capacity to take charge of public interests. The only experiment hitherto made has been successful. The government of Liberia is administered with as much skill as that of most of the States in our Union, and the republic is growing in importance among the nations of the earth. The Africans will learn soon enough to put confidence in Liberia, and to prefer their own administration to that of any other people in America.

3. Your "*rule of three*" will hardly work in reference to the developments of God's providence. "If now it has taken thirty-four years to place a colony of ten thousand on the coast of Africa, when can we reasonably calculate that our work will be done" with hundreds of thousands? Verily, by the Armstrong rule, no calculation would be "reasonable." Virginia herself could by ciphered out of her present civilization and glory, by writing down, for the basis of the problem, the original Jamestown efforts at colonization. The "rule of three," irrelevant as it has always been, will become less and less geometrical, "as ye see the day approaching." How will it work when " nations are born in a day?"

It must be admitted that, although the rule is unfair in such a discussion, no human sagacity can scan the problem of African colonization. It is certain, however, that many of our wisest men regard colonization as the most hopeful adjunct to emancipation. On the question of time, there is room for difference of opinion; and so there is, indeed, on all points. The late DR. ALEXANDER, than whom no man stood higher in Virginia for wisdom and far-reaching views, thus sums up his views of the capacity of Liberia to receive the coloured race of America : " If Liberia should continue to flourish and increase, it is *not so improbable*, as many suppose, that the *greater part* of the African race, now in this country, will, in the inscrutable dispensations of Providence, be restored to the country of their fathers." Some of our most distinguished political characters have expressed the same opinion.*

There are various providential aspects, which encourage large expectations from Liberian colonization, in its connection with the removal of American slavery, and which serve to show that an emancipation movement, of some kind, cannot be far off.

III. Besides hoping great things, and attempting great things, we should "look with holy anxiety at THE SIGNS OF THE TIMES." Providence is a quickening instructor.

1. One of the signs of the times is, *the general sentiment of the civilized world* in favour of measures of emancipation. Slavery has existed in the United States for two centuries, during which period it has been overruled, in many ways, for great good to the slaves. But can it long survive the pressure of public sentiment at home and abroad? When all Christian and civilized nations are opposed to its continuance, must it not, before long, adopt some active measures tending to its abolition?

2. Another sign of the times is, the demonstration of *African capability*, made by the Republic of Liberia. The light of this Republic spreads far into the future. It illuminates the vista of distant years, and cheers the heart of philanthropy with the sight of a great and rising nation. The moral power of the successful enterprise on the shores of Africa, is like the voice of God speaking to the children of Israel to "go forward."

3. *The exploration of Africa*, just at this period of her history, is another cheering sign for colonization. Preparations for a great work are going on for that dark continent. Whatever developes Africa's resources, is a token of good to her descendants everywhere. Elevate the continent, and the race is free. These explorations will serve, in part, to satisfy the public mind in reference to the healthfulness and fertility of the country, back from the sea, and its adaptation to all the purposes of colonization.

4. Another sign of approaching crisis, favourable to some important results, is in the *South* itself. After a long period of repose, it presents tokens of internal divisions, of excitement, and of extreme measures. The revival of the African slave-trade, which is a popular plan in six States, bids defiance to God and nations. The preparations, commenced in Maryland and elsewhere, to drive out the free blacks or reduce them to slavery; the movement to prohibit emancipation by legislative enactment; the laws against the instruction of the slaves; all the recent political ad-

---

* An enlightened advocate of colonization, as an adjunct to emancipation, need not maintain that the *whole* African race in this country must go to Liberia. Many of them will probably remain behind in this country, to struggle with adversity, and perhaps at last to die away. Dr. Alexander's language goes as far as is necessary to meet the case. "*The greater part* of the African race" will probably be restored to Africa.

vances of slavery, including the judicial decision denying the rights of citizenship to free blacks, and carrying slavery into the national territories; and especially the lowering of the tone of public sentiment on the whole subject of slavery and emancipation, to which even ministers have contributed: all this has the appearance of an impending crisis, and points to some great result in Divine Providence, in spite of all the opposition of man; yea, and by means of it!

5. The times magnify *Colonization as an instrument of civilization.* Behold the new States on the shores of the Pacific, and the rising kingdoms in Australia. Behold the millions who have peopled our own Western States. Colonization has never before displayed such power, or won triumphs so extensive and rapid. Nor has the black man ever attained such dignity as by emigrating to Africa. Colonization is one of the selected agencies of God to promote the civilization of the human race.

6. It also seems clear that God had some *special purpose of grace and goodness* to accomplish with the slave race, on a large scale. The Africans have been torn from their homes, brought to a land of liberty and religion, civilized and elevated here, to a good degree, and yet, when set free in the land, disowned as citizens, and subjected to a social and political condition, so disparaging as to preclude the hope of fulfilling their mission in America. Everything points to Africa as the field of their highest cultivation and usefulness.

7. The concurring providences of God throughout the earth are harbingers of *the times of renovation and of millennial glory.* The fulfilment of prophecy is at hand. Progress and revolution mark the age. The end is not distant, when " He, whose right it is, shall reign ;" and " Ethiopia shall stretch forth her hands unto God."

With signs like these flashing across the heavens, it is no time for the watchers of the African sky to sleep at their observatories; much less, if they are awake, is it a time to doubt. Providence calls upon the friends of the race to hope great things, and to attempt great things. It points to Liberian Colonization as the most hopeful scheme ever devised for the elevation of Africa's degraded children, and for their emancipation from the long American bondage. Work, and see! Trust, and try!

SECTION XII.—EFFECTS OF ENTERTAINING THIS EMANCIPATION SCHEME.

In your judgment, the discussion of emancipation is calculated to "do harm." Why, then, did my good brother introduce the question, and in a form that seemed to demand an answer? The whole discussion is evidently foreign from the original issues between us, as most readers readily see.

For myself, I do not believe, that a calm and Christian discussion of this vast social and political question will do any injury at all. It needs investigation. It requires it before God and man. The interests of the white race and of the black race, the welfare of the present and succeeding generations, conscience, political economy, safety, the public opinion of the civilized world, religion, Providence,—all invite serious attention to the question of emancipation. And why should a rational discussion interfere with "the religious instruction and gradual elevation of the African race?" Its natural effect, one would think, would be to stimulate effort in this very direction, at least with Christian and sober-minded people.

The Free States have, unquestionably, been remiss in their duties to the free coloured population. I confess, with shame, this neglect and injustice. Human nature is the same everywhere. The free blacks have, however, many privileges. They have access to public schools; they have churches in abundance; and if they could enjoy social equality, they would long ago have been "assimilated" in our communities. You ask, "Are you colonizing them in Africa?" I reply, that hitherto they have refused to go, notwithstanding the most earnest and persevering expostulations. The same class of fanatics who have urged immediate and universal emancipation at the South, have decried colonization at the North, and successfully resisted its claims among the free people of colour. There are evidences that a change of opinion is now silently making progress among them in favour of colonization. May God help us to do more in their behalf, and to roll away the reproach, of which you faithfully remind us, and for doing which I give you my thanks.

SECTION XIII.—THE WORK AND THE WAY.

There is no difference of opinion between us about the work and the way, although I believe that we ought to keep the end in view, as well as apply the means. Why work in the dark? The great obligation is the improvement of the slaves, their intellectual and moral elevation. The slaves, in my judgment, and, I suppose, in yours, ought to be taught the rudiments of learning. Our missionaries to the heathen place Christian schools among the effective instrumentalities of promoting religion and every good result. What can be gained by keeping the slaves in ignorance, it is difficult to conjecture. Ought not the Bible to be placed in their hands, in order that they may "search the Scriptures" and possess the opportunity of a more complete improvement of their rational powers? A committee, in their report to the Synod of South Carolina and Georgia, in 1833, state: "The proportion that read is infinitely small; and the Bible, so far as they can read it for themselves, is, to all intents, a sealed book." Since 1833, progress may have been made in the instruction of the slaves in the rudiments of knowledge. And yet, in view of the fact that several of the States, including Virginia, have, within this period, passed stringent laws prohibiting the slaves from being taught to read, it is difficult to ascertain the nature and extent of this progress, if indeed there be any. In some States, I fear there has been an interposition that leads to retrogradation.

You are right in saying that the most effectual way of promoting emancipation is "through the agency of a gradually ameliorating slavery, the amelioration taking place as the slaves are prepared to profit by it." What strikes a stranger, at the present time, is that the laws have, of late years, become more harsh, especially in the matter of instruction, than ever before. An "ameliorating slavery" would naturally *extend* the educational and general privileges of the slaves. Has there ever been any public legislative action having in view the enlightenment of the slaves? Might not Christian citizens accomplish much more in ameliorating the code, by enlarging the privileges of the slaves in conformity with the recommendations of Mr. Nott?

The remedial suggestions of Mr. Nott, understood to be received with favour by a number of gentlemen at the South, are of much value. If generally adopted, the work of amelioration would be carried forward with an increase of power altogether unknown in the annals of slave civilization. Among his admirable suggestions, which are generally elaborated with much good sense, are the following: "There may be supposed admissible in the progress of amelioration, first, some extension of franchises to those remaining slaves; and secondly, an opportunity of full emancipation to such as may choose it: thus giving to all some share in providing for their social well-being, and opening the path for individual progress and advancement."

An ameliorating system is the only, and the safest, way to emancipation; and in such a system, religious and moral instruction is the strongest element. The plan of emancipation we have been considering could have no prospect of a successful issue, unless, in the course of thirty years, a great advance could be made, under God, in the intellectual and social condition of the slaves. The intermediate work is Christian elevation; after that, emancipation.

I am far from undervaluing the general tendency of Southern civilization towards the improvement of the slaves. Great credit belongs to those of our self-denying brethren who have made special efforts in their own households and on neighbouring plantations. Let this work go on, and thousands of slaves will be prepared for freedom, in Liberia, in the course of another generation. This is the work, and this is the way!

SECTION XIV.—THE CHURCH AND ADVISORY TESTIMONY.

After this long digression, of your own seeking, I return to the original topic of the relation of the Church to emancipation. The Church has a right to *enjoin* the performance of all the relative duties specified in the Scriptures, and to give general *counsel*, or *testimony*, in regard to the termination of the relation itself, as a moral and lawful end.

Why a right to give counsel? Because, as I have attempted to show, the relation being abnormal and exceptional, its ultimate dissolution is fairly inferred, as a moral duty, from the general spirit and principles of the word of God. So far as the dissolution of the relation requires the action of the State, the Church has no right to meddle with it in any form, either as to the plan, or the time. The Church has simply the right to advise and urge her members to prepare their slaves for freedom, as soon as Providence shall open the way for it.

Why may not the Church *enjoin* emancipation? Because slaveholding being right or wrong, according to circumstances, the Church can neither give a specific rule of permanent and universal obligation, nor can it take cognizance of the circumstances of each particular case, which must be adjudicated by the mind and conscience of each individual under his responsibility to God.

The Church, therefore, whilst it cannot prescribe political measures of emancipation, or the time of emancipation, has a perfect right to say to its members, as our General Assembly did, in 1818:

"We earnestly exhort them to *continue, and, if possible, to increase* their exertions to effect a total abolition of slavery. We exhort them to suffer no greater delay to take place in this most interesting concern, than a regard to the public welfare truly and indispensably demands."

"And we, at the same time, exhort others to *forbear harsh censures*, and uncharitable reflections on their brethren, who unhappily live among slaves, whom they cannot immediately set free; but who are *really using all of their influence and all their endeavours* to bring them into a state of freedom, *as soon as a door for it can be safely opened.*"

Or, as the Synod of Virginia declared in 1802:

"We consider it the indispensable duty of all who hold slaves to *prepare, by a suitable education, the young among them for a state of freedom, and to liberate them as soon as they shall appear to be duly qualified for that high privilege.*"

In thus maintaining the right of the Church to give advisory testimony, there is scarcely need to add, that the Church is bound to proceed with the wisdom which should ever characterize a court of the Lord Jesus Christ.

SECTION XV.—THE THIRD LETTER. HISTORY OF ANTI-SLAVERY
OPINIONS.

1. I do not conceive that my third letter was based upon the slightest misapprehension. The whole strain of Bishop Hopkins's apology for slavery implies, like your own, that the institution may lawfully exist among a people, forever, without any concern. This I do not believe; and this the Christian Church has not believed, either in earlier or later times. I protest against such doctrine, in however guarded language it may be expressed or concealed.

In the time of Chrysostom, who flourished after Constantine, about A.D. 400, emancipation was encouraged throughout the Empire; more so than my brother Armstrong seems to encourage it now, in the interval of fourteen centuries. There is no reason to infer from Chrysostom's fanciful interpretation of 1 Cor. 7 : 21, that he was an advocate of the perpetuity of slavery. In some respects, that distant age was in advance of our own.

2. You think that in two instances I confound things that differ. (1.) But I did not understand you as saying that the Christian anti-slavery philanthropists of England were infidels, but simply that they acted *quoad hoc* on infidel principles. I proved that their principles were not those of infidelity; that such an idea was preposterous.* (2.) Nor did I confound slaveholding with the African slave-trade. The paragraphs from Mr. Bancroft's history embraced both subjects, so that one could not be well separated from the other. Besides, the traffic and the system sustain a close relation to each other. The abettors of perpetual slavery are always prone to defend the slave-trade, as is lamentably witnessed at the present time, in the extreme South.

SECTION XVI.—CONCLUDING REMARKS.

On reviewing our respective positions on this interesting question, I am confirmed in the correctness of those with which I set out, viz. : that "slaveholding is right or wrong according to circumstances;" that the General Assembly had a right to exhort the members of the Church to prepare their slaves for freedom whenever Providence should open the door for it; that the history of anti-slavery opinions shows that the Church has never regarded slavery as an institution to be perpetuated; that it is wise for us, as *citizens*, to examine the question of emancipation in all its bearings; and that the border States, if no others, might advantageously commence the work speedily, on the plan of a prospective scheme, with Liberian colonization as its adjunct.

* HOBBES, one of the leaders of infidelity, maintained that every man being by nature at war with every man, the one has a perpetual right to reduce the other to servitude, when he can accomplish the end.

On the other hand, if I do not misunderstand you, you have taken the following positions: 1. "Slaveholding is not a sin in the sight of God." 2. The Church has no right even to advise her members to elevate their slaves with a view to their freedom, and that the testimonies of the General Assembly, down to 1845, were wrong, and ought never to have been uttered. 3. Slaveholding has always existed in the Church without any reproach, from the earliest times, until Christian philanthropy, adopting the principles of Infidelity, has lately agitated the matter. 4. It is expedient to do nothing in the way of emancipation at present, *if*, indeed, the slaves are ever to be free; and the South had better not send any more slaves to Liberia until the North has sent its free blacks.

By the expression of these sentiments, I fear that, without intending it, you have lowered the tone of public sentiment wherever your influence extends, and have impaired the obligations of conscientious Christians on this great subject. John Randolph declared in Congress, " Sir, I envy not the heart nor the head of that man from the North, who rises here to defend slavery from principle." This remark has no direct application, of course, to yourself; but many readers, I fear, will claim, in your behalf, the credit of doing the very thing that John Randolph denounced.

I agree with you about the evils of the course of the fanatical abolitionists; and not any more than yourself do I desire to unite my honour with their assembly.*

I stand upon the good old ground, occupied by the Presbyterian Church from time immemorial. Believing it to be scriptural ground, I have endeavoured to defend it; and shall, by God's grace, continue to defend it on all fit occasions, against extreme views either at the North or at the South. I further believe that my beloved brethren at the South occupy, in the main, the same conservative position,—a position which has enabled our Church to maintain her scriptural character and her integrity. I do not expect that my brethren, either at the North or South, will agree with me in all the side issues about plans of emancipation, which you have thrown into the argument without any logical authority, and to which I have replied according to the best light given me.

Praying for spiritual blessings upon Africa and her descendants, and that the cause of truth, liberty, and righteousness may prevail from shore to shore,

I am yours fraternally,
C. Van Rensselaer.

---

* Notwithstanding Dr. Armstrong's strong condemnation of the abolitionists, he practically, but unintentionally, adopts two of their leading principles. 1. He discourages, at least for a long period, the emancipation of slaves, with a view of sending them to Liberia. So far as this generation is concerned, Dr. Armstrong and the abolitionists are, on this point, at unity. 2. He maintains that Africa ought not to be regarded as the country and home of the coloured race; but that America is as much their home as it is his or mine. This is a favourite and fundamental principle of the abolitionists, from which *they* argue emancipation *upon the soil.*

NOTE. DR. BAXTER ON SLAVERY.

Since writing the foregoing Article, a friend has forwarded to the Presbyterian Historical Society, Dr. Baxter's pamphlet on Slavery. I have read, with great interest and satisfaction, this remarkable production of my revered theological instructor. It breathes the spirit of his great soul.

1. The principles of Dr. Baxter's pamphlet are *not at all inconsistent* with the Assembly's testimony of 1818, which he had a share in preparing and adopting. The general views are coincident with those of that immortal document, with such difference only as was naturally to be expected in looking at the subject from a different stand-point.

2. In the statement of the *doctrine of slavery*, Dr. Baxter fully agrees with me, as will be seen by the following quotations from his pamphlet:

"The relation of the master is lawful, as long as the *circumstances of the case* make slavery necessary." p. 5.

"There is no consistent ground of opposing abolition, without asserting that the relation of master is *right or wrong according to circumstances,* and that the *examination of our circumstances* is necessary to ascertain whether or not it be consistent with our duty." pp. 9, 10.

"It therefore appears plain, that the Apostle determines the relation of master to be a lawful relation. [Here Dr. Armstrong would have stopped, but Dr. Baxter adds.] I only mean that slavery is lawful, whilst *necessary;* or that it is lawful to hold slaves, whilst this is the *best thing that can be done for them.*" p. 15.

"I believe that the true ground of Scripture, and of sound philosophy, as to this subject, is, that slavery·is lawful in the sight of Heaven, whilst *the character of the slave makes it necessary.*" p. 23.

Dr. Armstrong will see that my doctrine of *circumstances,* and nothing else, was in the mind of Dr. Baxter. This was the Assembly's doctrine of 1818. Dr. Baxter was no wiser in 1836, "eighteen years afterwards," because he was scripturally wise in 1818. I have a firmer persuasion than ever, that the great mass of my brethren at the South agree with Dr. Baxter, and not with Dr. Armstrong.

3. Dr. Baxter does not hesitate to speak out, like a man and a Christian, against the idea of the perpetuity of slavery.

"For my part, I do not believe that the system of slavery will or can be perpetual in this country." p. 16.

"Christianity in its future progress through the world, with greater power than has heretofore been witnessed, I have no doubt will banish slavery from the face of the whole earth." p. 17.

"The application of Christian principles to both master and servant, will hasten the day of general emancipation." p. 23.

Dr. Baxter uses no *ifs,* like a man afraid of his shadow, but boldly declares the common conviction of the Christian, and even political, world in regard to the desirableness and certainty of ultimate emancipation.

4. Dr. Baxter's pamphlet is specially directed against the abolition doctrine of immediate emancipation; and his object is to show that slavery can only be abolished by preparing the slaves for freedom under the influences of Christianity. I find nothing in the pamphlet on the question of Church testimony. There is no doubt, in my own mind, that he adhered to his views of 1818, on this, as on other points. God bless his memory and example! "Being dead, he yet speaketh."

INDEX.